An Angry Person's Journey to Inner Peace

Finding Freedom from Emotional Hell

Alicia Pierre

An Angry Person's Journey to Inner Peace: Finding Freedom from Emotional Hell

Disclaimer: The events in this book are from the author's memories and the author's perspective. Some names and characteristics have been changed to protect the identities of those involved, and some dialogue has been recreated.

Neither the author nor the publisher assumes any responsibility or liability whatsoever on behalf of the consumer or reader of this material. Any perceived slight of any individual or organization is purely unintentional.

The resources in this book are for informational purposes only and should not be used to replace the specialized training and professional discretion of a health care or mental health professional.

Neither the author nor the publisher can be held responsible for the use of the information provided in this book. Please always consult a trained professional before making any decision regarding treatment of yourself or others.

ISBN: 979-8-9883584-0-4 (paperback)

Dedication

To my husband, Motty, thank you for your grace and forgiveness, and especially for a love I didn't know could exist until you showed it to me-a love topped only by that of Jesus Christ, our Lord and Savior. To Him to be the glory.

To my daughter, Veronica. When you were born, something inside me began to heal in a way I didn't know I needed. I will forever cherish our early years together, just as I treasure all the moments we have now to reconnect. I am so proud of the young woman you have become. You have created a life of love, community, and friendship for yourself that warms my heart. Thank you for your grace, forgiveness, and love. Your heart-felt poems and sweet notes of encouragement mean the world to me.

To my son, Michelangelo. Your life has shown me that the most important things in this world are people and relationships. Thank you for shining a light into the darkness of my heart and helping all of us heal. Your name means messenger who is like God, and you have been that messenger. The light of your life has had, and will continue to have, a significant impact on the world around you. You have changed this place in a way I could not have imagined or planned for. You are a treasure.

Both of you kids have a belly-busting sense of humor and dry wit that I adore experiencing. Alone you're great; together, you're amazing!

~ Thank you all for sharing this life with me. ~

Contents

Contents

About This Book

This book is for those who feel stuck in emotional cycles of anger, fear, sadness, control, and manipulation. This book is for those who feel down and defeated, those who don't know, or don't believe, that God loves them unconditionally, those whose hearts are numb and who can easily feel anger, but for whom other emotions such as joy, don't come often or easily. This book is for those who want to change but are unsure how to process their thoughts and feelings, how to view themselves, or how to move forward.

This book is written for those who have grown up in church or who know *about* God but have had difficulty developing a personal relationship with Jesus Christ due to abuse or trauma they've faced in life. This book is *not* written from a "poor me" perspective, but is however, written with the acknowledgment that we have to look at what has happened in our lives-what mindsets we've developed as a result-and what steps can be taken to form new ways of seeing ourselves so that we can experience more joy and peace.

This book is for all of us who do what we think we *should* but have no real fire or drive inside to do it. This book is for those who want to find freedom from pain, anger, and emotional hell, those who want to feel peace in their hearts, but don't know where to begin. If you can relate, you're not alone. This book is the extension of my hand to a brother or sister, saying, "I'll walk back into my hell to help you get free from yours." For God's glory and your freedom in Christ Jesus, may you know the peace *only He can give*.

"But I will restore you to health and heal your wounds,

declares the Lord…."

~Jeremiah 30:1

Introduction

Recently I was watching a college football game and listening to the announcers. They were excited, energetic, and positive as they gave their perspectives on the abilities of the different players. They said things like: "This young man has explosive energy and is a powerful runner!" "That young man's coaches have said he's one to keep an eye on; he's a great asset to the team!" "I really love to see this young man in action-the way he moves, his vision for seeing plays-he's phenomenal!"

I thought, "I wonder how these players would feel and how it might affect their perceptions of themselves if they knew all these great things the announcers are saying about them!"

Then I had an epiphany: our Heavenly Father, The Creator of the Universe, wants us to have a proper perception of ourselves based on His unconditional love for us! He wants us to know He is in the "sound booth" of Heaven cheering us on! Ephesians 2:10 says, "For we are God's *workmanship* [emphasis added], created in Christ Jesus to do good works, which God prepared in advance for us to do." He made us and gives us good work to do!

He wants us to know Psalm 91:11 that says, "…he will command his angels concerning you to guard you in all your ways…," and Romans 8:28, which says, "And we know in all things God works for the good of those who love him, who have been called according to his purpose."

But when we come from a background of abuse, we don't immediately identify with positive words spoken about us. We're used to negativity. We're used to being downcast and broken. We're used to things *not* working out in our favor.

Abuse causes us to believe the lie that we're not worthy to be loved and that our value depends on how others treat us, what we look like, what we own, or what we can do.

Deep down, I didn't know, or didn't believe, I was worthy of God's love. I was jealous of those who seemed to easily proclaim, "I'm a daughter (or child) of the King." Those words didn't resonate inside my heart. The concept felt foreign to me, like a language I couldn't understand, words that had no meaning to me.

I couldn't relate to the statement, "…a *child* of the King." I felt it was for others, but somehow not for me. I had been rejected, abandoned, and emotionally abused by human parents. How could I believe that God (my Heavenly Father) loves me, takes care of me, promises to never leave me?

My relationship with my Creator was confusing and tarnished with lies I believed about myself.

On one occasion, I remember telling my husband that I felt that God is angry, that He's mean, and waiting to punish us. (Used to feeling ashamed of myself, my brain filtered everything through the lens of feeling ashamed of myself, and-you won't be surprised by this(!)-I continued to feel ashamed of myself! This is why it's so important to be honest with ourselves about what we think and feel and begin to look at the ideas we hold that are holding us back-which is my purpose for writing, so keep reading!)

The next day, I opened my Bible "randomly" to Nehemiah Chapter Nine. The first verse I saw was Nehemiah 9:17 which says, "...But you are a forgiving God, gracious and compassionate, slow to anger and abounding in love. Therefore you did not desert them."

Thinking back to that moment, I am moved to tears by the overwhelming love and mercy of God. His nature is such a sharp contrast to our human nature, and the opposite of what I was accustomed to feeling inside. I needed Him and He was there for me, ready to teach me more about Who He is.

Nehemiah Chapter Nine talks about the patience of God with His people, His compassion and forgiveness. Even when God's people turned from Him (repeatedly!) and began to worship other gods, when they suffered because of their actions and were oppressed, they cried out to their Creator, and He heard them and delivered them from their enemies-*every time*.

Jeremiah 29:13 says, "You will seek me and find me when you seek me with all your heart."

My opening "randomly" (which wasn't random at all, but was the grace, mercy, and love of God!) to Nehemiah Nine is one example of how God rewards those who seek Him. I had sincere concerns and questions, and because my heart's desire was to know the truth of Who He is, He was faithful, and He answered me.

You may be thinking, "All of this *sounds* great and ideal, but what if I don't *feel* anything?" Or, "What if all I feel is rage?" I've been there!

A little over twenty years ago, a friend of mine asked me, "How is your heart doing?" I thought, "What? What do mean? My heart? I don't think about my heart."

Not wanting to say *that*, I assumed what she wanted to hear! I answered, "It's good. How's yours?"

Truthfully, the most familiarity I had with my heart at the time is that I could feel it beat, creating the pulse at my wrist. Beyond that, the beautiful, electrical organ behind my chest wall was a stranger to me. Literally, thoughts of what I was feeling "in my heart" caused me confusion. I felt a blockage there I couldn't get past.

I had a couple predominate feelings-the main one anger, the other fear.

The rage I felt, always just below the surface, was the result of a chaotic, emotionally abusive environment in which my safety depended upon the moods of my caregivers. Their good mood meant I was safe. A bad mood meant their anger might be directed at me.

I learned to be externally focused, searching for my worth and value in how others treated me. I learned to both fear people and want their approval. I learned to take on responsibility for other people's moods and behaviors.

I felt rejected, ashamed, that no matter what I was doing it wasn't the "right" thing; I was never good enough. There were constantly negative judgments about me and disgusted, disappointed looks. I felt guilty, lonely, confused, lost. I was so accustomed to people finding a reason not to like me that I eventually began to start conversations with anger and sarcasm because I knew rejection was coming! My anger protected me.

People who are chronically angry are hurt, scared people. Used to negative, unpleasant experiences with others, we get tired of feeling terrible about ourselves. We grow weary of being shunned when our hearts crave love and acceptance. Not knowing how to manage the pain and chaos inside, we find ourselves in a perpetual state of rage.

Spoiler alert: I'm not going to tell you to stop being angry. Anger can be useful. Anger serves to keep us safe when we're in danger. Anger can give us the drive we need to make positive changes in our lives. Anger is a signal to us that something isn't right and needs to be addressed.

This isn't the type of anger that's a problem. Problem anger is that which causes us to explode in rage, yelling, being emotionally or otherwise abusive. Problem anger causes us to block off our hearts and look outside ourselves to find love and acceptance, not knowing, and not being able to *feel*, that unconditional love (God) lives in our hearts! And has been there since *before the creation of the world* (see Ephesians 1:4)!

My purpose is to show how emotional abuse, rejection, and abandonment left me externally focused, feeling insecure, anxious, unworthy, ashamed, and disapproved of, pursuing (false) safety and temporary approval in my ability to control and manipulate people, but how, through an honest assessment of-and taking responsibility for-my thoughts and feelings (no matter how socially unacceptable!), and by seeking my Creator, I discovered something other than anger and fear in my heart, and came to know inner peace and freedom from emotional hell.

At the end of each chapter, I offer you *Mindsets to Move Forward*, which are practical tools for daily life. These are sometimes short affirmations, other times more detailed ideas, but always information I have found important for my journey.

Know that you are not alone. The Creator of the Universe loves you more than you may think or believe, with a love that is unconditional. You don't have to earn His love. You don't have to prove yourself worthy. He doesn't take His love from us when we "mess up"!

My prayer is that you would know Him and believe that His love is for you-*exactly* as you are today, right here in this moment. It doesn't matter what you've ever said or done at any time in your life- or what has ever been said or done to you. You are unconditionally loved and accepted by *The Creator of the Universe*! That's a big deal!

My encouragement is to look to God for your self-worth, acceptance, and approval. Believe in your heart He's there and begin to talk to Him. Tell Him your thoughts, hopes, concerns, dreams. He already knows anyway! But in talking to Him, you establish your relationship with Him. Ask Him to lead you by His Holy Spirit to the books, the people, the podcasts, the online messages of hope and healing that will build your faith in who He says you are and in His love for you.

Ask God the hard questions. Go to His Word for answers. Romans 10:17 says, "Consequently, faith comes from hearing the message, and the message is heard through the word of Christ."

If something doesn't sit right with you, research it. Press into the question. Like my husband says, "Peel back the onion." See what's driving the discomfort and curiosity. (Often looking at another translation of The Bible brings greater clarity.)

When you're ready, ask Him to guide you to a church that teaches from the Bible. Read your Bible daily. Seek Him. Jesus said in Matthew 7:8, "For everyone who asks receives; he who seeks finds; and to him who knocks, the door will be opened." When you do these things, you're knocking on the door of your heart and like Jesus said, "...the door will be opened."

Tips for Triggers

As you begin this book, I want to give you some techniques to deal with intense feelings. I discuss sensitive issues (see ** at the end of this section) and want you to be prepared in case you find any topics triggering.

We can't avoid triggers, but we can develop ways to manage our feelings when faced with them. In future chapters, I'll discuss additional, healthy ways to manage difficult emotions. For now, here are a few tactics that I've found helpful on my journey:

For anger:

*Scream into a pillow or silent scream by opening your mouth as wide as you can. Squeeze your eyes shut, bunch up your face, and pretend you are screaming as loudly as you can. Surprisingly effective! (One night when I was alone in my car, I knelt down in the back seat and screamed-loudly-to release pent up rage. A neighbor must have heard because he came outside and looked around. When he went back into his house, I went back into mine! Whatever it takes!)

*Punch your bed or a heavy sack.

~ Before doing the following breath exercise, please consult your healthcare provider. ~

*Exhale completely by blowing all your air out before taking a deep breath in. Try breathing in through your nose and out through your mouth. Think, "Smell the roses; blow out the candles." It's helpful at times to make your exhale longer than your inhale. If you have a hard time getting a full breath in, try taking two breaths in before exhaling.

*Go for a walk or run.
*Do push-ups, jumping jacks, or mountain climbers.
*Say your ABCs or count backward.

For sadness:

*Cry.
*Journal your feelings, write a poem, paint, draw.
*Same breath technique described above.
*Go for a walk.
*Talk to a friend, a counselor, or pastor, or even your pet.

This is a basic list to get you started. If at any time you have thoughts of harming yourself or someone else, please call 911 if you're in the United States. Additionally, the National Mental Health and Crisis Hotline number in the United States is 988.

I've found that there are some books I'm more comfortable reading at home, by myself, with adequate privacy to feel and to process my emotions. This may be the case for you in reading this book. Create a safe space for yourself to experience what is necessary for you to heal.

**Emotional abuse, violence. Chapter 22 talks about child sexual abuse and gives resources for support, as well as practical steps to apply right away if a child tells you they've been abused. Chapter 24 talks about anxiety, depression, and suicidal ideation.

Important Contacts

National Domestic Violence Hotline available 24/7

(Languages: English, Spanish and over 200 other languages)

1-800-799-7233

thehotline.org

For thoughts of harming yourself or others

911

Or go to nearest Emergency Room

National Mental Health and Suicide Crisis Lifeline

988

988lifeline.org

Always Remember:

You are unconditionally loved by

The Creator of the Universe.

YOU ARE NOT ALONE

Chapter 1

Loss of Connection with Yourself

In the Beginning

It's interesting what happens in the hearts and minds of children who have come to expect loving, predictable responses from their caregivers. Their needs are addressed consistently and with patience and logic. These children develop a healthy nervous (or stress response) system and feel *securely attached* to the people who provide their care. They feel calm, stable, and have developed a sense of safety and security. They know they're worthy of time, attention, and love. They feel valued, accepted, and approved of. They know home is a safe place, a firm foundation, and they have a healthy perception of themselves and other people.

They love themselves because they were treated with love. They're confident in their abilities because they were made to feel capable. They can think for themselves because they had a peaceful and safe environment that allowed for higher levels of brain functioning-those needed for logic, reasoning, planning. They know that if they fall or if they fail, they'll be encouraged to get up and try again. They feel courageous and competent and believe that people are generally kind and loving.

Contrast this with the chaos of *insecure attachment*, which is the result of emotional-and other forms of-abuse. Your environment is unpredictable, unsettling. Caregivers might be pleasant sometimes, angry, and aggressive other times. There's no consistency. You don't know what to expect, so you don't develop trust in your relationships. Your stress response is always on. You may startle easily and be unable to relax, to think, to imagine. You develop ways to try to control and manipulate your surroundings to maintain stability and predictability. You learn that peace is found outside yourself and is dependent upon the moods, words, and actions of other people. You learn to depend on others for your sense of self because you never got to know *you*. You're afraid of people. You've been rejected, devalued, and disapproved of, so you feel ashamed and don't make eye contact with others. You feel guilt and humiliation. You don't have a firm foundation of inner peace and self-confidence. You believe the world and the people in it are scary and unpredictable because that's what was learned at home.

Ideally, our stress response system is in place to help us fight off danger, flee from it, or freeze in place until the threat has passed. All these responses to danger are normal. What's not normal is when this system is perpetually on and we find ourselves in a constant state of fight, flight, or freeze as happens in an abusive or dangerous environment.

Our bodies are consistently flooded with stress hormones that can lower our immune function making us more susceptible to illness and disease; our cardiovascular systems are wracked with substances that can cause clogged blood vessels leading to stroke or heart failure; we don't think clearly and may "zone out" easily.[1] Teachers or coaches may have told us to "pay attention" or they may have complained to our parents that we "don't listen" or that we have to be given instructions repeatedly. The rational, logical parts of our brains don't function well in a chronic stress state, making learning and memory exceedingly difficult.

While the physiological effects of chronic stress can be tragic, one of the worst consequences that occurs when we're raised in an abusive environment is that we haven't had the opportunity to get to know ourselves.

When we've spent most of our time in fight, flight, or freeze mode, we've learned to be externally focused, constantly monitoring whether our environment is safe. Our sense of stability and security was dependent upon the shifting moods of our caregivers. If they were in a good mood, we were probably suspicious because outcomes were unpredictable. They might be happy in the moment, but we never knew when their mood would change. We were prisoners to fear of other people's emotions, so we didn't have the opportunity to feel peace, to relax and to learn who we are-what we like or dislike, what causes a spark in our hearts. We developed the habit of looking to others for how we should feel about ourselves. We likely felt guilty because we were made to feel responsible for other people's emotions and behavior. From this guilt, we feel ashamed of who we think we are.

We haven't experienced stability at home; therefore, we lack identity, safety, security, and self-confidence. We've learned that we're not worthy to be treated with calm and patience. Instead of feeling accepted, we feel rejected. We don't feel valued. We don't have a healthy self-concept because *we do not know who we are.*

What Rejection Does

Rejection tells us there's something wrong with us; we don't measure up to standards; we aren't good enough. Rejection sends the message that we're not valuable, not worth people's positive attention, which causes us to feel ashamed of ourselves. Those who don't understand how we've been treated may think that we're "just shy."

As a child, and even into my early twenties, I had a small, quiet, and timid voice. I wouldn't look people in the eye. I didn't want attention but felt that people were constantly watching me and making negative judgments. I'd been conditioned to think that whatever I did wasn't the right thing to do or wasn't good enough, so I started to look for my worth and value in what I was praised for-my performance at school, or as an athlete, and in my appearance.

At some point when I was very young and without my conscious awareness of what was happening, I began to stuff my emotions deep inside my chest. They were too heavy for me to think about or feel. I lacked knowledge of what healthy relationships look like and how to process emotions that come up therein.

My environment was chaotic, fear-filled, and controlling. There were moments of softness, but the pervasive messages I got were that I should be ashamed of myself; nothing I did was right; I wasn't what I 'should be.' I wasn't worthy of time, attention, patience, unconditional love, and acceptance. These thoughts had become my core beliefs.

Our self-concept (or self-perception), how we view ourselves, is the result of how others have treated us, especially in our formative years when we are, by design, the most impressionable. As children, we're sensitive to other's reactions and responses to us. In the presence of healthy caregivers, we learn to have a positive self-image.

We feel safe with them, and we learn to have compassion, grace, mercy, patience, and love for ourselves because they've modeled those traits.

On the other hand, if adults frequently acted angry and frustrated with us, we began to feel rejected, not good enough, and that we're inherently flawed. We learned that our value and our worth is contingent upon the negative moods and behaviors of others.

When we don't have a healthy self-perception, we grasp anything we can to feel good about ourselves. We desperately seek external acceptance and approval. Because the world judges our worth based on our appearance, our performance (i.e., how good we are at school, a job, or sports), or our possessions (the more expensive our stuff is, the more valuable the world says we are), we learn to *do* more of the things, and strive to *get* more of the things, that the world gives us acceptance and approval for. We learn to feel we're valid and worthy only if we look good, can perform well, or if we have expensive things.

External Motivations

Performance

I've been athletic since I was a child. On one occasion, I remember helping my grandpa and my grandparents' friends gather firewood. I did my best to get attention from the adults for carrying the heaviest log I could find! I was also praised by my elementary school gym coach for my physical capabilities, and remained active in sports throughout high school, so, after a year of college, when the possibility of joining the Army came up, I wasn't concerned about the physical requirements.

I also wasn't overly troubled by the idea of drill sergeants yelling at me, because by this time, I was adept at blocking out angry people. (I admit, I felt a little differently when I arrived at basic training!)

Accustomed to performing for acceptance, overall I did well in the Army. The idea of being told where to go and what to do appealed to me. I lacked inner guidance and found comfort in taking direction from others. I was a great rule follower (because I wanted to be validated), so I got *more* acceptance for performance!

In the Army, I didn't have to think too much or feel too much. I simply had to perform. I was rewarded for being "a good soldier." I liked the accolades and kept performing.

About two and half years into my three-year contract, I was ready for change. I became tired of being told where to go and what to do. A familiar feeling of having little control over my life returned. I felt trapped and was ready to be free.

When I finished my obligation to the Army, I struggled to readjust to civilian life. I wanted to show my military ID card to cashiers when I shopped at civilian stores, as this is customary in military establishments. Your Armed Forces ID tells people who you are, proves you have a right to be there. Who was I if my ID card no longer told me (and everyone else) who I am? Where was my sense of value and worth? I could no longer perform for acceptance the way I did on active duty. After all, no one in the civilian world cares how many push-ups and sit-ups you can do or what your time is on a two-mile run!

Appearance

Because I had nothing else on which to base my identity, when I was a little girl, if someone told me I was pretty, I felt I was worth something and would be treated well. I felt valuable and worthy to be loved since I was "pretty." I literally had no other ground to stand on. Logical thinking didn't enter my mind until much later in life. I was great at using my brain for people pleasing (seeking approval from others) but forget about logic! Nope. It was nonexistent.

My world inside and out was governed by emotions-mine and those of the people around me. With a wall over my heart for protection, rational, meaningful conversation wasn't possible. Growing up, I had friends (thankfully!) who were content to hang out and be goofy with me, watching movies or running around in the back yard, but I had no clue what healthy relationships truly looked like.

The belief that our worth and value come from our appearance doesn't create solid ground on which to base our self-confidence or identity. But I did base my worth and value on my appearance, so a bad hair day meant my day was ruined! If I wasn't worthy because of my appearance, what else did I have?

I had no identity aside from other's opinions of me. I lived to go to school and see the cute boy I had my eye on hoping he'd return my admiration so I could feel good about myself. I was never focused on *my* heart and what was important to *me*. All I cared about was getting approval and validation from others. When I didn't get it, or had it but then lost it, I struggled to feel a sense of security and self-worth. Everything I thought of myself was based on the reactions of other people–factors outside myself that I could not control.

Possessions

While my clothes weren't what the popular or "cool kids" wore, I didn't struggle as much with identity in this area as I did with my physical appearance and performance.

Regardless of which form of external approval we have leaned on to feel validated, none of them are a firm foundation on which to develop a healthy self-perception or identity. Why not? Looks fade, an injury can forever change our physical abilities, and money and other possessions can be gone in an instant.

So, the question becomes: On what then do we base our sense of self-worth and our identity?

A Solid Foundation

No one may have told you this before-or you may have been told and not believed it: You are worthy of love, and you are accepted by God. Yes, *You.* Exactly as you are right now in this very moment. How do I know this? God, The Creator of the Universe, breathed His Life into you (see Genesis 2:7). Genesis 1:31 says that all He created is *very good.* He said that He knew you before you were formed in your mother's womb (see Jeremiah 1:5). He said He knew you before the creation of the world (see Ephesians 1:4)! He said that you are in this world, but not of this world (see John 17:16).

What does that mean? That means your identity doesn't come from the things the world says it does. It means you're a spirit having a human experience. Sounds good in theory, right? But what happens when our human experience hasn't been great? What happens when instead of being treated as a precious child, known by The Creator of the Universe, and formed by Him in our mother's womb, we're abused, abandoned, neglected, treated like we don't matter, treated like we're not worthy, and not enough?

What happens is we begin to believe lies. The younger we are when the abuse occurs, the deeper the lies get inside us and shape our thinking, words, and behavior.

Even if we're not conscious of our beliefs, our thoughts, words, and behaviors reflect them.

What God Says

Developing a healthy self-concept begins when we *say* about ourselves what God, The Creator of the Universe, Our Creator, says about us. Why? He made us! And He made us *in His image*. Because He tells us the power of life and death is in the tongue (see Proverbs 18:21), and because God *spoke* the world into existence (see Genesis 1), we know *our words* have the power to create–or to destroy!

Isaiah 55:11 says, "so is my word that goes out from my mouth: It will not return to me empty, but will accomplish what I desire and achieve the purpose for which I sent it." All of us have experienced hurtful words that leave us feeling weak, defeated, powerless, and downcast, and all of us have received life-giving words of encouragement that give us hope and joy. Psalm 16:24 says, "Pleasant words are a honeycomb, sweet to the soul and healing to the bones."

To begin to create the image of ourselves God has of us, we must use *our words* to speak what He says about us in *His Word.* If I'm going to know the truth of who I am, it makes sense to go to my Source of Life!

It's important to note that we may not *feel* anything at first when we say, for example, "I am God's friend," (see James 2:23), but as we continue to speak Our Creator's words, we begin to replace negative, untrue thoughts about ourselves. By speaking life, we're using the Sword of the Spirit, the Word of God (see Ephesians 6:17), to cut down the lies we've believed.

Psalms 1:2 tells us to meditate on God's Word and Proverbs 7:3 says to write God's commands on the tablet of our hearts. How do we write God's commands on the tablet of our hearts? We read His Word. We think about it. We *meditate* on it. And when we do this, Jesus tells us in Matthew 12:34, "…out of the overflow of the heart the mouth speaks." The words we hear (and read)-what we *think* about-have power. What we put into our hearts and minds and what we *say* about ourselves, is vital to establishing our identity in who God says we are.

My purpose is to show you there is hope. You can think and feel differently about yourself. You don't have to feel down, ashamed, unworthy, or unlovable.

You can begin to turn around your thinking by putting good seed (God's Word) into the soil of your mind. Your value and worth are not dependent upon what any other human has ever said or done to you or what you've ever said or done that does not line up with what The CREATOR OF THE UNIVERSE says about you.

Romans 8:31 says, "If God is for you who can be against you?" The answer is *no one*. When the Creator of the Universe tells me that He's on my team, the game changes. The Bible, His Word, says the battle belongs to the Lord (see 2 Chronicles 20:15). How? He sent his Son, Jesus Christ, not to condemn (disapprove of) the world, but to save us (see John 3:17)-to approve of us, to effectively remind us of who we are-to remove the separation between us and God.

God sent Jesus to Earth to show us our identity is not found in what the world says it is. The world tells us that our value and self-worth are based on our appearance, performance, or possessions. God wants to remind us we're valued and worthy because *He* made us. When we forget who we are because of the abuses we've suffered, our pain, anger, and sadness can make us feel separated from Our Creator. Jesus came to remind us that we're not what happened to us.

You aren't your anger, your sadness, your hurt, sorrow, depression, anxiety. You're not the ugly comments made about you or the hurtful things that have been done to you. You're a child of the living God.

Our human parents may have failed us in many ways. They may have said they loved us, but humans are flawed, imperfect, and unfortunately, sometimes blatantly abusive. I, too, am a parent and failed in many ways, but we have a Heavenly Father who does not fail us (see Lamentations 3:22). He cannot lie to us (see Titus 1:2). He is the same yesterday, today, and forever and His love for us does not change (see Hebrews 13:8). God is our Rock (see Psalm 62:2) and Firm Foundation (see Matthew 7:24-25). It can be hard to believe this, but faith comes by hearing the Word of God (see Romans 10:17). So, keep going!

Mindsets to Move Forward

*Take a deep breath and tell yourself, "I am loved by The Creator of the Universe exactly as I am-right now in this very moment. It does not matter what I look like, what I can do, or what I have. I am loved by God." (John 3:16)

*God knows me and accepts me (Jeremiah 1:5 and Genesis 1:31).

*I am a spirit having a human experience (John 17:16); therefore, I am not my appearance; I am not my possessions, and my worth is not found in my accomplishments.

*God looks at my heart. 1 Samuel 16:7 says, "...The Lord does not look at the things man looks at. Man looks at the outward appearance, but the Lord looks at the heart."

*God is for me (Romans 8:31).

*God's love for me does not change (Hebrews 13:8).

Chapter 2

The Chaos Within: Power and Control

Many of my early childhood experiences left me feeling powerless and afraid. My parents fought with each other, shouted, and threw things. I remember an incident when I was three or four years old in which I was made to eat my cereal off the floor after I'd accidentally spilled it. In tears, I picked it up one piece at a time while my angry father stood behind me, yelling. Chronic stress took a toll on my heart, mind, and body. Recalling this event, I can feel the physical effects. My stomach is tight, and the back of my head feels tense. I feel hot with fear, anger, and shame.

I wish deeply I could state with pride that I never made my children feel like that, but I regret with all my heart that many times I made them feel the same way. While I never yelled at them for spilling cereal, I yelled often and sometimes cussed. Like my caregivers, I was frequently angry and impatient. As we go along, I'll get into more detail regarding the mindsets I held that were driving my behavior-mindsets that I wasn't consciously aware of at the time.

As a child, my requests for assistance were often met with frustration and intolerance. I cried a lot. No one ever said, "She's such a happy child!" People say this as if the child has everything to do with their emotional state! I've heard adults praise kids who are cheerful and smiley. It's illogical to me that children are rewarded for being happy because children are products of their environment-what they witness daily and what's said and done to them-the positive and the negative.

Because of my experiences, even as a nurse, I've struggled with anxiety when I need to see my primary care provider. (It's not because I don't like needles! I was an infusion nurse for several years and loved giving shots and starting IVs. My patients said I was good at it, and I don't mind being on the receiving end!) But in asking for assistance, I've sometimes felt transported back to the child who needed help and didn't get it.

Not knowing what response I might get when I'm vulnerable, and not wanting to feel helpless, I've put off going to my doctor. Sitting in the room waiting to be seen has made me feel like a victim before anything has even happened! This is obviously because I *was* a victim when I was a child. As a child, I was powerless to determine the outcome of an interaction, or ensure I got what I needed, and at times this mindset creeps in when I'm in a similar situation. (Of course, we need to keep our healthcare appointments, and we're no longer a defenseless party in the resolution of our requests for help! See Chapter 8 for information on empowerment in conversation, mutual respect, and assertive communication.)

The anxious thoughts I have about what *might* happen never materialize! Like my son wisely told me once, "Why not wait until something *actually* happens and deal with it then instead of worrying about what *might* happen?" Great advice! (In fact, in this chapter's *Mindsets to Move Forward* and in future chapters, I'll discuss the supernatural protection available to us when we proactively praise God!)

Regardless of the circumstances, we can all relate to being made to feel powerless. In a hostile and tense environment, I learned to look outside myself for my sense of safety, security, and peace. Depending on the moods of my caregivers, I felt I could relax a little or I became anxious if they were angry because I didn't know what would happen.

My environment was predominately chaotic and busy. Inside I felt anxious and out-of-control. I learned early on how to use my sense of humor to diffuse tension among adults. I wanted to feel safe and the only way I could do that was to control other people's moods or the circumstances.

From childhood, I took on responsibility for other people's behavior. I tried to smooth things out, prevent yelling, protect myself from harm. I'd become controlling and manipulative because my safety depended on other people's moods. I took accountability for what I never should have taken ownership of-other people's behavior!

Ways We Control

Physical Environment

Having been emotionally abused, I didn't have a sense of inner peace or security. I didn't feel okay about myself. I didn't feel safe, and I needed something to put confidence in. I had no control over the inner hell and turmoil I constantly felt, so I looked outside myself for something I could hold on to and over which I could excerpt my influence.

Out of this desperate search for a sense of stability and control, when I was in elementary school, I used to stand at the light switch in my bedroom and before leaving, I would recite the Bible verse my grandma had hanging on the wall above the switch. As I recited the verse, I would visually inspect the room moving my eyes from left to right over every one of the trinkets on my dresser. Then I would look at my pillow, my blankets-making sure everything was in perfect order before I shut the light out and left. (I can still see myself, hand on the light switch scanning the room from left to right. For some reason, one of the figures on my dresser was a ceramic donkey. I don't know why I had that!)

If one thing were out of place, I would leave the light switch, move it the one-quarter inch or so that I felt it was off, and head back to the light to start the process all over again.

I also had a habit of counting constantly in my head-while walking down the hall, up and down the stairs, while brushing my teeth. During this time in my life, I used to feel that my hands were "grody" all the time. (Yes, "grody" is a word!) I specifically remember approaching one of my fourth-grade teachers at her desk and saying, "I need to go to the bathroom to wash my hands." She asked me why. I responded, "They feel 'grody'." She said, "Grody?" I said, "Yes." She allowed me to go, and I remember being deeply satisfied seeing the soap suds form on my hands as I washed away the disgusting feeling!

In the fourth grade, I washed my hands so much that the skin on them became extremely dry and cracked. It even bled sometimes! Mom and grandma got me a pair of pretty, white, satin gloves and petroleum jelly to coat my hands with and place the gloves over at night.

My hands eventually healed, and at some point, I stopped standing at my light switch, obsessively reciting the Bible verse while checking for order.

As for the constant counting, I recall one afternoon when I was brushing my teeth, and counting in my head as usual, I got very angry. I was exhausted with the perpetually running internal counter. I remember mentally shouting to myself, "STOP IT! STOP COUNTING!"

For some reason-that maybe a neuroscientist could explain-the internal burst of anger was enough to sever the connection or break the neurotransmitter signals in my brain that had triggered my obsessive need to count.

My preoccupation with a need for order, the counting, and the hand washing were all ways I was grasping for a sense of safety and security. Inside I felt chaos, confusion, and disorder, so I controlled-and put into order-what I could! While I no longer do any of these things obsessively, I am a person who craves *routine*, a sequence of actions regularly followed.[1]

In his 2014 book, *The Body Keeps the Score: Brain, Mind, and Body in the Healing of Trauma*, Dr. Bessel van der Kolk, discusses the importance of synchronicity and rhythm [routine] in helping people regulate after suffering traumatic events.[2]

As a child, I was absolutely dysregulated. Constantly afraid of what an angry adult might say or do, my fear drove me to take responsibility for their behavior. It is traumatic, terrifying, and exceedingly stressful to live with people who don't take ownership of their words and actions. I felt disorder and confusion inside as a result of the chronic stress. In doing what came naturally to me-arranging my things in a perfect order, counting, and obsessively washing my hands-I was subconsciously seeking the synchronicity and rhythm, or routine, I needed to help start calming the chaos within.

I'm not suggesting you take up counting or develop an obsessive need to wash your hands and maintain order in your environment! However, a routine can be very useful in creating harmony in your life. In fact, science shows routine can have measurable benefits to our mental and physical health![3]

Hyperactive Energy and Being Overly Talkative

The out-of-control, chaos I felt inside sometimes came out as hyper energy. I remember being erratic and talkative as a child. (And I've caught myself doing this as an adult!) I understand now that this was my attempt to hold people's attention so I could control both what was happening around me, and other people's opinions of me. With the focus on me, I ensured that my audience thought I was funny and entertaining. If they were laughing and engaged, they weren't angry!

And if I was able to make them laugh then, in my mind, I had their acceptance and approval. (I didn't know it at the time, but I was giving away my self-respect to win external validation.)

I'd developed the belief that if I didn't have people's attention, I'd be forgotten, left out, talked about behind my back, made fun of, or otherwise judged negatively. If I weren't controlling the dialog, I believed people would decide they didn't like me. I wouldn't have their approval.

Additionally, if people saw me as fun and entertaining, no one would ask me what the *look on my face* means! I've always struggled with "the look on my face." (Or, to put it in a way that is more kind to myself, *other people* have had an issue with the look on my face!) Knowing part of my background, I'm sure you won't be surprised to hear that I didn't smile much as a child, teenager, or even well into my adult years. In fact, when I was a little girl, one of my uncles used to call me "grouch"! A girl in high school echoed the sentiment I'd heard from others many times before when she asked me one day, "What's that look for?" I said, "What do you mean?" She said, "You look mad." I remember thinking, "I don't know what my face is doing! This is how I look!" My face reflected what I was feeling inside. How could it not! Even more reason to use my sense of humor to control people's perceptions of me! (There will be more about the *look on my face* in Chapter 15!)

People Pleasing

When I was nervous that someone might be in a bad mood, I asked them questions about topics I knew they were interested in. I didn't care what the answer was. I was assessing their demeanor. I needed them to be happy so that I was safe. If they were *not* in a good mood, I took it upon myself to remedy the situation. Again, something I never should have felt responsible for-other people's moods!

I controlled to feel safe, and I controlled because I wanted people's acceptance and approval. I didn't feel valued or worthy of acceptance as I was. In my mind, I had to *do* something to earn approval or ensure I would get it, so I tried to govern others' thoughts and feelings. I gave people compliments or smiled and greeted them to influence their perception of me. I needed to be seen positively, so that I'd be liked, and so I wouldn't be the target of anyone's negative judgments or hostility.

I used to try to get people to like me by agreeing with their opinions. I wouldn't even allow myself time to think about what they were saying! I would simply agree because I wanted their approval!

When we act because we want someone to like us, our behavior is not authentic; it's a control tactic.

Before you agree with someone's opinion, allow yourself time to process what they've said. If you don't have an immediate answer, say, "I need to think on that." *We show respect for ourselves and are more respected by others when we don't quickly give away our approval to get someone else's.*

If you're going to smile and greet someone, do it from a place of sincerity in your heart and not because you're looking for validation. (There is certainly an art of communication that can build business [and personal] relationships. My objective is to help you overcome fear of people and needing too much approval, so the focus here is primarily learning self-respect and assertive communication.)

In my people pleasing days, my feelings (and the resultant look on my face) hadn't won me any social approval, and at the time, I needed it, so I did my best to mask my emotions. But in trying to please people and get *their* acceptance, I was dishonoring *myself* by not accepting the reality of my inner turmoil.

Needing to be The Best

Sometimes we seek control of people's perceptions of us by needing to be the smartest person in the room. Afraid of appearing incompetent, we feel valid if we're the only one who has the answer or the only one who knows how to do the thing that needs doing. Those who base their worth on their ability to perform sometimes judge others as "incompetent" to boost themselves up.

When our value is found in external things, the approval we get from people for how well we perform, our sense of self-worth is threatened if other people are good at what we're good at (or even better than we are)!

This mindset is one of the reasons people gossip, trying to tear down those they perceive as a threat to their position. (Sometimes we feel threatened and jealous because we don't know our true worth and value is in our identity as a child of God-unconditionally loved and approved of by Him. And sometimes we feel threatened and jealous because we're not being treated with the dignity and respect that we should be!)

Perfection

When I was around seven years old, I remember wanting to have a "perfect" day. In my seven-year-old mind, this translated to a day in which my brother and sister didn't bother me! I thought that if they left me alone, there wouldn't be a chance that we'd fight, thus ruining my plans to display perfect behavior.

I remember sitting by myself a lot that day! But the feeling of being "perfect" didn't last long. One of my siblings said or did something I didn't like, and I got my grandma involved to let her know they were messing up my perfect day!

What was I searching for? I wanted to feel safe and secure in who I was. I wanted to feel good about myself. I felt that if I behaved perfectly, that I *was* perfect and therefore worthy of acceptance and approval. To seven-year-old me, perfect behavior meant I deserved to be treated well.

Perfection is rooted in the lie that we have to perform for acceptance, and we have to *earn* love. This lie negates the truth that God loved us *before we even knew Him*! He loves us freely and unconditionally.

The Joy Stealer or Daisy Downer

Joy stealers/Daisy Downers are people who habitually do not share in our excitement about things. They want us to be excited when it has something to do with them, but if it's our excitement and happiness, they act like Eeyore from *Winne-the-Pooh*![4] Instead of being happy that we're happy, they act downcast, monotone, pitiful, and defeated-which serves to accomplish the goal of their behavior: to keep all the attention on them, so they feel in control, and therefore, safe.

They want people to ask them, "What's wrong?" They want others to feel responsible for their emotional state. They try to make sure that if they feel down, you feel down too! (This is different from actual depression. This is a form of control and manipulation.)

The Daisy Downer is also the person who, when you're in a room enjoying yourself (watching TV or reading a book for example), they come in and start slamming cupboards and drawers, sighing, making it obvious that they're working while you're relaxing, and they don't like it! (I know because I've done this, and I've seen others do it!) Their behavior is an attempt to steal your joy by making you feel guilty.

Joy stealers cause us to be on guard when we'd prefer to open our hearts and be happy and excited or simply relaxed! Instead, we feel guilted, stifled, and ashamed when they're around. We approach these people with caution and keep our tone of voice slightly defeated because we normally feel defeated after we've talked to them!

People who take responsibility for their own thoughts, feelings, and behaviors can readily share in someone else's excitement and joy-even if the reason for the celebration has *nothing* to do with them!

People who are joy stealers cannot control us if we're enjoying ourselves, but when they see they can affect our mood by dragging us down, this is how they keep "the ball in their court" so to speak.

Daisy Downers have legitimate issues, but until they take responsibility for what they're feeling, they believe others are responsible for helping them feel better. They lack a sense of stability and security within themselves and look for it in their ability to control and manipulate the people in their environment.

People who take responsibility for their emotions recognize that *their* feelings are *their* job to take care of and they can share in a friend's joy even when they're dealing with their own difficulties.

When we recognize what's ours to deal with and what belongs to others, we not only protect ourselves from burn out (taking on emotions that don't belong to us), but also, we're not attempting to control others (by getting them to take responsibility for our emotions).

How We Got Here

Abuse causes us to believe the lie that we should feel ashamed, guilty, and responsible for other people's moods and behavior. It causes us to feel that we're not worthy, valuable, or loved. It causes us to look outside ourselves for what has been in us before the creation of the world-God.

God in us is our Source of life-giving power to feel peace, love, joy, stability, safety, and security, but abuse separates us from our identity in Him and causes us to stay stuck in anger, fear, shame, and internal chaos, not knowing the firm foundation of Our Creator's unconditional love for us.

Hosea 4:6 says, "my people are destroyed from lack of knowledge."

When we've been disempowered by the pain and shame of rejection and abuse, we lack knowledge of God's acceptance and approval. We lack a feeling of inner power and control. Unaware that authentic power and peace come from *inside* us, we seek power and peace in our ability to control, or get approval from, others.

The definitions of power and control are almost identical. Power is the capacity or ability to direct or influence the behavior of others or the course of events.[5] Control is the power to influence or direct people's behavior or the course of events.[6]

These definitions suggest that empowerment is based on external factors-controlling other people and circumstances. It's the kind of power we may be accustomed to, but it's not reliable. External control isn't a firm foundation on which to base our self-worth and identity because we're trying to control something we were never meant to control-other people!

My hyperactive controlling worked occasionally but it wasn't sustainable. People on the receiving end of this energy often feel suffocated, pressured, not free to have their own thoughts or make their own assessments about a situation. They feel anxious and exhausted because the hyperenergetic person is taking up all their psychological space-preventing them from thinking and feeling what they choose.

Chaotic, obnoxious behavior robs other people of their peace to listen to what's going on inside their hearts and minds. I was overactive and controlling because I'd learned that if people are left to have their own thoughts and feelings, I'm not safe. I learned they will find something-something about me, something I had or had not done, or even something unrelated to me-to be angry about and I would be the target of that anger.

When my control tactics worked to ward off an angry outburst or gain temporary acceptance, I felt calmer inside. I was at peace for the moment. I felt empowered that I had influence on other people and circumstances.

But external power and control aren't a source of lasting peace, safety, and security because we cannot truly govern the actions of any other person. And we're not meant to! The Bible tells us to be *self*-controlled (see 1 Peter 5:8), not *others* controlled!

Anything we rely on outside of God in us is not a firm foundation. A firm foundation is found in self-control, empowerment from within, based on the knowledge of God's unchanging love for us. But many of us are versed in exerting control over *others* to feel empowered, because this is what we've learned. External control happens when: we feel overly responsible for someone else's behavior and we're enabling them to dodge the consequences of their actions; when we want someone to feel responsible for how *we* behave; or when we want approval and validation.

I was raised thinking you get people to respect you and do what you tell them by using anger to intimidate them to act. This is codependency because the parties in the relationship look to each other for their sense of safety, security, and inner peace-one person controls the other and feels falsely and temporarily empowered, and the other person gets approval and validation for complying with the controller's wishes.

One person is scary and angry, and the other person is submissive and afraid. Or one person is pitiful and downcast and the other feels responsible to help them feel better. Whatever control tactics are used, in a codependent relationship, those involved are looking for peace in their ability to control people and circumstances outside of themselves.

It's important to note that the roles of controller and controlee can flip flop, so the relationship becomes a to-and-fro dance of manipulation, playing on each other's fear of abandonment, emotional, or physical harm, or guilt about abusive behavior.

When abuse has left us feeling disempowered, we seek power the way we saw others get it. We use our energy to control who and what we can. When we see that our words and actions influence others, we get a false sense of security. We feel empowered because we see that we have an impact on those around us.

This can be particularly intoxicating to those of us who come from an abusive environment because we were the ones who felt powerless and afraid. Not knowing any other way, we feel empowered and in control by using anger, pity, or other coercive strategies to get people to do what we want.

But God never intended us to make others feel scared or control people in any way for us to feel empowered. 2 Timothy 1:7 says, "For God did not give us a spirit of timidity, but a spirit of power, of love and of *self*-discipline [emphasis added]."

We're to trust in Him, lean on Him, look to Him and not to other people for our self-empowerment, our self-control. Psalm 121:1-2 says, "I lift up my eyes to the hills-where does my help come from? My help comes from the Lord, the maker of heaven and earth."

This doesn't mean we never need people. It means we don't *depend* on others for what we're meant to get from Our Creator. People's moods and behaviors change, but Our Creator is the same yesterday, today and forever. Our empowerment, our solid foundation, comes from the peace, safety, and security we have knowing Who Our God is and that He loves us and lives in us.

True control is self-control, not the control of others. Proverbs 25:28 says, "Like a city whose walls are broken down is a man who lacks self-control."

When we feel responsible for other people's moods, words, and behavior, because our emotional or physical safety is dependent upon those factors, or when we want others to feel responsible for *us*, our city walls get broken down. We're looking outside ourselves for empowerment. We're externally focused, controlling and manipulating other people for our sense of safety, security, and inner peace.

As a child who was externally focused, I learned to protect abusers from the repercussions of their actions by trying to keep the peace, change their mood by telling a joke, or trying to help them find a solution to what made them angry. I was powerless, especially in my youth, to change an angry person's behavior so I adapted to survive. I became an *enabler*, because at the time, it was impossible to hold anyone accountable.

I learned to control and manipulate to avoid rejection, shame, fear, loneliness, and to feel validated and approved. When my caregivers treated me with anger and impatience, I thought their behavior meant that something was wrong with me. I felt unworthy, rejected, and powerless.

In a hostile, angry environment, all my energy was externally focused, spent thinking about other people and what their mood was. All my thoughts revolved around keeping angry people happy.

My identity was completely wrapped up in how other people treated me, what they thought of me, and what I felt were their expectations of me. I'd learned to equate other people's behavior with my perception of myself. The shame I felt because of how I was treated made me feel guilty and responsible for things I am not responsible for-other people! Shame, anxiety, fear, and guilt made me believe that everyone else's moods and actions were the result of something I had or had not done. I was constantly externally focused on gaining control instead of aware that my self-control, my self-empowerment, comes from God's love for me.

Mindsets to Move Forward

When we don't know we're unconditionally loved by God, we lack a sense of inner peace, safety, and security. In short, we feel disempowered, and we find ourselves trying to take power from-or we become overly responsible for-other people.

The following is a short list of ways people try to take power from others:

*Making us feel "less than" or not good enough somehow
*Making us feel responsible for their emotions
*Making us question our worth by:
- *being condescending
- *never giving approval or praise
- *withholding affection, smiles, nods of acceptance
- *belittling
- *making fun of or using the guise of a "joke" to get away with racism, sexism, or a judgmental attitude
- *using anger to intimidate and control
- *name calling; telling us we're "bad"
- *any form of abuse
- *comparing us to others to show we come up short in some way

Comparison is the death of happiness, and it's a lie that our worth is found in anything but God's love for us!

It can be a sign that someone is trying to take our power when we feel like we have to defend ourselves whenever they're around.

Notice if you or others are using any of these tactics and remind yourself that your power doesn't have to be taken and you don't have to take power from others. Each of us is valid, worthy, and loved right now just as we are. Find a way to communicate that preserves the dignity and self-worth of all involved. Not everything needs to be talked about! Sometimes we need to journal it out.

We *can* control other people with fear, anger, self-pity, hyperactive energy, negative judgments, and so on, but we *aren't meant* to get our sense of power from our ability to control others.

True power (inner peace, safety, and security) comes from knowing we are unconditionally loved, accepted, and approved of by The Creator of the Universe.

We get a false sense of power, a temporary "fix" when we can get others to do what we want, but external control is not a firm foundation. External control relies on other people. External control is not founded in our relationship with God in us.

When I catch myself being hyper and talking way too much, I usually recognize my behavior right away and will look at what thoughts are driving me to seek control in that moment. Obviously, I'm looking for acceptance, but my goal is to discover the reason I want it. I ask myself, "What am I afraid will happen if I don't have control?"

Needing people's approval and using hyperactive control, for years, kept me from getting in touch with my heart. It kept me from knowing myself and it prevented others from knowing me. Because I needed to be liked, I wasn't willing to show anyone my fear, anger, or sadness! I didn't truly get to know anyone else's heart either because I was busy using up all the energy in the room to ensure people were making positive assessments about me!

These revelations made me wonder: What if I had people in my life who weren't afraid of the real me? What if I had people who love me and accept me as I am-even if the look on my face sometimes does mean that I'm not in the best of moods?! What would happen if I let go of my need to control what others are thinking of me?

Answer: I could develop authentic relationships! Some people might misjudge the look on my face, but if they cared about my heart, we would have a conversation about it and, possibly, establish a friendship.

If you notice you use hyperactive control like I did (and sometimes do!), try another approach. As my daughter would say, "Dive deep." Dive deep into silence. There's peace in silence. Authenticity lives there. Bravery lives there. It takes courage to be silent while others might misjudge, reject, gossip about, or ostracize you, but people who do that are not your people!

Exodus 14:14 says, "God will fight for you; you need only to be still."

God's power to keep us at peace prevails when we're appropriately silent. What do I mean by *appropriately silent*? It means that sometimes speaking up is best and we need to use wisdom to determine when that is.

People whose identity comes from God's approval and unconditional love for them-as demonstrated by key people in their lives-don't feel intimidated by greatness. They celebrate it, learn from it, and get better themselves, because they know God doesn't show favoritism (see Acts 10:35). In other words, He's the Father of all of us who accept Him and follow His way (see John 1:12). What's possible for one of us is possible for any of us if we believe it is!

Knowing God loves us unconditionally, we know we don't need to be the best at everything to be valid. We don't need everyone to see things our way because we know we're approved of and accepted by Our Creator. Our energy becomes expansive instead of clogged up and shut down when we celebrate others, but we cannot celebrate others if we don't love and respect ourselves. Love and self-respect will come as we continue to look at the mindsets that got us where we are and as we keep learning what God says about us.

If you're the person who knows how to do the thing that needs doing, empower someone else and teach what you know! You may think, "Well, no one showed me how to do it! I had to figure it out on my own!" Be a bigger person and share your knowledge. It might feel good to give!

It's easier to maintain my identity in who God says I am when I pay attention to how I feel when listening to music, television, or other social media. Some of the messages therein can start to poison the well of our minds with suggestions that we have to look a certain way, have the latest technology, or do particular things to be acceptable or worthy. Songs that objectify our bodies (women or men), can make us doubt our worth and value if we don't measure up to the specifications put forth in the lyrics.

Living in this world, it can be quite easy to believe lies that our worth is found in what we own, what we look like, or what we can do. There's nothing wrong with looking our best or doing our best, but when we start to measure our *value* by those things, we're not focused on our true identity-that we're accepted, approved of, and *unconditionally* loved by God.

Consider trying a Christian radio station and notice if you feel differently inside. Psalm 22:3 says, "God inhabits the praises of his people." When we praise Him, we feel *Him* in our hearts and His presence silences the voices that tell us we don't measure up. We're not looking outward for external approval, so our city walls remain fortified!

Protect your heart from people who have a habit of being condescending or jealous of you. Sometimes it's better for our mental health to keep our ideas for projects to ourselves until the product is finished. This keeps our hearts and minds focused on what God has put in us instead of fear of other people's opinions or approval. My husband doesn't struggle as much with people pleasing as I have in life, so for him, he'll do what's in his heart regardless of other people's opinions. Know for yourself what you're comfortable sharing with others. Everyone has different boundaries. We show ourselves respect when we adhere to ours.

Sometimes there's no way to avoid people who try to steal our power. We don't have to give it to them, but it can be very annoying to be constantly plagued with criticism, condescending remarks, gossip, and so on. Own your power and go to the source of the problem.

I've been around older, or more experienced, nurses who've been in the profession longer than I have and, because they were bullied when they became nurses, want to do the same. They say things and use a tone of voice suggesting that the newer nurse is incompetent, unqualified, will never do well at the job. When this has happened to me, I've said, "The comments and tone aren't necessary. I'm here to learn and I would appreciate mutual respect." They may not like me because I set a boundary, but they usually have a respectful attitude going forward. I spent too many years giving away my power, afraid of people not liking me, wanting acceptance and approval, that

I have an extremely low tolerance for people's efforts to disempower me.

Some people will like us, some will not. That's life! We can all be mutually respectful regardless of our opinions of each other, *and*, we don't have to justify our dislike of a person by trying to get everyone else to dislike them! As my husband would say, "That's petty." Go about your business and stay out of theirs. 1 Thessalonians 4:11 says, "…mind your own business…"!

Pray for people you encounter in daily life. I have a better attitude and more peaceful interactions with people after I've prayed for them. I ask God to be with them and their families. In fact, Matthew 5:43-45 says, "You have heard that it was said, 'Love your neighbor and hate your enemy.' But I tell you, love your enemies and pray for those who persecute you, that you may be children of your Father in heaven...."

Protect your peace by renewing your mind daily to your identity as a child of God. When we do this, we remind ourselves not to look for our value and worth in how other people treat us or in their acceptance, approval, or lack thereof. Your power to feel inner peace, safety, and security, your self-control, comes from God's unconditional love for you.

Chapter 3

Grace for Parenting: Generational Fear & Anger

A parent's responsibility is to model God's love for their children. This is what Proverbs 22:6 means that says, "Train [or start] a child in the way he should go, and when he is old he will not turn from it." When our parents model God's love for us, we learn to love ourselves, and the natural result is a desire to love others. Unfortunately, when I became a parent, I didn't have an understanding of God's unconditional love for me, and I didn't love myself.

Lacking the firm foundation (inner peace, safety, and security) that comes from knowing God approves of us and loves us unconditionally, I sought peace, safety, and security in my ability to control people and circumstances.

I was emotionally immature. I was codependent on my children, meaning my self-worth depended on their behavior. I was peaceful and calm when they did as I asked, but I was angry and impatient when they didn't. (Deep down, I was afraid I'd be judged for my children's choices.)

Key caregivers in my childhood were consistently angry and impatient as well. I lived in fear and learned to feel responsible for their moods and actions. I learned to control and manipulate to feel safe and secure. When authority figures were happy, I was treated well. I felt safe.

My caregivers' conduct showed me that to get children to respect you and comply with your wishes, you use anger. When people are afraid of you, they feel ashamed and responsible for your behavior, and you can control them. As if I'd been a sponge as a child, when I became a parent, these methods oozed out of me without my conscious awareness. I was repeating the cycle of codependency and emotional abuse I'd absorbed in childhood-without even thinking about it.

When my kids didn't do as I asked, I became angry quickly and yelled. Feeling guilty for yelling, I gave them extra attention, trying to make up for the hurt I'd caused. Not knowing how to heal the root of my anger, my gentleness didn't last long, and I resorted again to yelling as a form of discipline, which doesn't teach anything but fear, shame, and performance for acceptance. It teaches external motivation. It teaches that to be worthy of kindness and patience-to maintain people's love and acceptance-you have to behave perfectly.

My inconsistent actions with my children sent them the message that love is conditional and based on their performance.

As a codependent parent, I took on too much responsibility for my children's moods and behavior and I made them feel responsible for mine. I believed that their emotional state was always the result of something I had or had not said or done. And my actions were intended to make them feel that my mood was because of what they had or had not said or done!

This dysfunctional way of thinking keeps all parties from being accountable for themselves and makes them *overly* accountable for everyone else! In this unhealthy environment, everyone blames each other for their moods and actions, and no one takes ownership of themselves. It's the dance of codependency that secures the relationships.

Codependency is reliant upon one person feeling *responsible* for another. In other words, if I can get someone to feel they're accountable, or are the *reason*, for my emotions and my actions, I can control them-but only if they need my acceptance and approval.

By design, our children are *meant* to need our acceptance and approval. To withhold it to get them to change their behavior is fear-based control and manipulation, which teaches kids to be externally motivated. It teaches them that our love for them is a condition of their behavior. Loving with conditions teaches fear, unwarranted guilt, and shame.

Instead of teaching my children internal motivation and self-control by empowering them with self-love, I had inadvertently-through my impatience and anger-taught them control, manipulation, and external motivation. (Thankfully, both of my children are much more emotionally mature in their late teens and early twenties than I was when I was raising them, and they know this isn't healthy behavior.)

How do we teach our children internal motivation and responsibility for their moods and behaviors? We model responsibility for ours. We *talk* about our feelings instead of *acting* them out.

I didn't realize for many years that I wasn't taking responsibility for my emotions. All I knew was that I was angry, and I wanted other people to know it, feel responsible for it, and tend to it-making me feel better. If people did what I wanted them to do, I was at peace. I felt in control. God knows I had no sense of inner control or stability, so having a sense of external control soothed me.

Again, we can control people who need our approval if we can make them feel responsible for our emotions and actions. This is how I learned relationships work: I'm responsible for your moods and you're responsible for mine. It's a tango of control, manipulation, and misplaced responsibility.

As a young parent, I was largely on autopilot and only aware years later of the reasons for my behavior, and how deeply I was hurting my family.

I needed their acceptance and approval, and I needed them to want mine. There was a part of me that believed if I didn't control them, they wouldn't need me or love me, so I made them feel *responsible* for me. Because when you feel responsible for something, you take care of it. You don't abandon something you feel responsible for. You pour your time and energy into it. You give it your attention. You make sure it's doing well.

These were things I'd needed from my caregivers in childhood. Because I didn't know I was loved and worthy exactly as I was, and because I didn't know it was unnecessary to control and manipulate people to get them to love me, I was using control and manipulation to get my childhood needs met in my relationships with my children and husband. And I was not consciously aware I was doing this! By making them feel responsible for my moods and by acting out my emotions, I set up a dynamic in which my family had to parent, or caretake, me. (Caretaking is meant for children or other people who don't have the ability to care for themselves.)

When I was living this dysfunctional pattern of behavior, I was unaware of the reasons I felt out-of-control and angry much of the time. I came to realize later that I didn't feel taken care of as a child (when it's healthy for other people to take care of you), and I longed to feel that.

It wasn't that I set out consciously thinking, "I'm going to slam cupboards and drawers and make people afraid, so they'll pay attention to me and do what I want them to, because when they take responsibility for me, I feel better. I feel taken care of." I was acting from a place of misery that I didn't know how to change. I was seeking inner peace and felt it (only fleetingly) when I was controlling others.

I didn't know how to be in relationships in which I took responsibility for my moods and behaviors and everyone else took responsibility for theirs.

I was afraid to let go of my control of my family. I believed that if I wasn't controlling them, they wouldn't love me or want to have a relationship with me.

I didn't know it then, but inside I was desperate for a sense of safety, security, and knowledge that I am unconditionally loved and accepted.

Mindsets to Move Forward

Your parents or caregivers may have abandoned you physically or emotionally. You may have desperately needed them, and they didn't come through for you. You may have suffered tremendously because they let you down. They dropped the ball. They didn't protect you when you needed a protector. They didn't fight for you when you needed someone stronger and more capable than yourself to shield you from harm. You needed emotionally mature parents, but they hadn't yet healed their childhood wounds when you came along, so you didn't get wise, mature caregivers. You may have felt more like you were the parent and they were the children.

It hurts. Deeply. Grieve your losses. Your anger is justified.

Know that your human parents are just that- human. You have a Heavenly Father Who promises in His Word that He will never leave you or forsake you. Psalm 28:10 says, "Though my father and mother forsake me, the Lord will receive me." Psalm 68:5 says that God is, "A father to the fatherless…."

*He is your shelter in life's storms.

*He's as close to you as the heart in your chest.

*He loves you so much that He suffered and died for you.

*There is no greater love than that which He has for you.

*You are worthy.

*You are loved and accepted exactly as you are.

In Hebrews 13:5 (Amp.), God says, "'…I will never [under any circumstances] desert you [nor give you up nor leave you without support, nor will I in any degree leave you helpless], nor will I forsake or let you down or relax my hold on you [assuredly not]!"

In Joshua 1:5 (Amp.) God says, "…I will not fail you or abandon you."

Practical Parenting

We can't do better until we know better, so we need to be educated about what children are, and are not, capable of understanding at different ages and developmental abilities. It frustrates me to see parents punish their children for developmentally appropriate behavior. For example, your nine-month-old child *will* drop things off their highchair-on purpose! It's normal! Don't smack their hands when they continue to throw their pacifier onto the floor after you have handed it back to them five times! They're learning about cause and effect. When we're knowledgeable about the *reasons* for our children's behaviors, we're empowered to respond with logic.

Research parenting methods, especially, if, like me, all you've known is codependency. There's no shame in getting help. In fact, we show that we're self-aware and want better for our children when we admit our areas of weakness. But don't stay weak! Get educated!

We can be angry about a *behavior* and not take it out on our kids or make them feel responsible for our emotions. What does this do? This keeps ownership for the action with the individual. We don't try to scare, guilt, shame, or humiliate our child to get them to change their behavior. In other words, we don't control and manipulate. From a place of self-control, we can calmly and logically ask for the behavior change we want, and when necessary, we can give calm, logical, age-appropriate consequences. This helps kids learn to have an *inner* locus of control instead of being externally motivated by anxiety and fear.

Ownership for Self

When we act out our feelings, slamming or throwing things, we're not taking responsibility for ourselves. The message we're sending is that if those around us don't want our anger turned on them, *they* must act to change *our* mood. *They* must say or do something to bring *our* behavior back under control. In this way, we're using fear to manipulate people into taking undue responsibility for us.

If we can make other people feel *responsible* for our emotions and behavior, we can *control* them, and we feel taken care of, but God never meant for us to control others and not take responsibility for ourselves!

Know what you are and are not responsible for. When beginning to heal from over-responsibility for others, it can be very uncomfortable watching people help themselves out of their own struggles. It's hard to sit back and realize, "I'm responsible for me, and you're responsible for you."

In the past, I was easily baited by people who acted out their emotions, especially anger. Because of my experiences, I automatically felt obligated to take responsibility for their mood. I wanted to say or do something to fix it! Now, I do my best not to entertain baiting behavior. Because of the work I've done to take ownership of my emotions, I'm able to maintain a mental and spiritual separation between what I am and what I am not responsible for. When necessary, I'll say, "Will you please *talk* about your feelings instead of *acting* them out?" Or to keep ownership of the behavior with the individual responsible, I'll say, "You seem to be slamming things a lot." What does this do? It keeps the person responsible for their behavior and prevents me from taking ownership of what I am *not* accountable for-other people's actions!

Develop a mindset of *self-control* from the knowledge that you are loved unconditionally by The Creator of the Universe, and you don't need to control and manipulate others to feel empowered, taken care of, or loved.

Repeat to yourself (and out loud when necessary), "I'm responsible for me, and you're responsible for you."

However, if you say or do something hurtful to someone, *you* are responsible for hurting their feelings. Don't say or do ugly things to people then tell them you can't help how they feel! That's emotional abuse. It's sick and wrong. I've witnessed this, and it infuriates me!

By talking out our emotions, we set our children free from feeling responsible for us. We set them free from our control and manipulation. We set them free from fear that they have to perform for our love-our patience, kindness, goodness, gentleness, and *self*-control. We set them free from thinking, "If I can just make mom laugh, she'll be happy and treat me well." When we take ownership of our emotions and actions, we teach our kids that our love for them is not contingent upon their behavior or our mood.

All of us need someone to love us and to feel that our worth is not tied to our appearance, performance, or possessions. In other words, we need to feel loved without conditions. Because we cannot give to our children what we don't have ourselves, practice loving yourself exactly as you are. God does! Be patient and kind to yourself.

Jesus was gentle and humble in Spirit, and He welcomed children to Him. Even if we haven't had this experience with our own parents, we can pray and ask God to make our hearts gentle toward our children.

Grace for ALL Our Mistakes

If you have regrets about your parenting failures, I want to share with you what my therapist said to me: "It's time you start showing yourself some grace. You did the best you could with what you had at the time. It's the first time you were a parent, and you didn't have a healthy model to follow."

The definition of grace (in the Christian belief) is the *free and unmerited* [emphasis added] favor of God ….[1] We can't earn it and we don't deserve it, but He gives it! Thank God for grace!

2 Corinthians 7:10 says, "Godly sorrow brings repentance…." The definition of repent is to feel or express sincere regret or remorse about one's wrongdoing or sin.[2] I feel deep regret and remorse for my words and actions toward my children; I have repented, and I've asked my children to forgive me. It's time I started forgiving myself!

Chapter 4

Echoes from the Past: Reasons for my Behavior

"Have I not commanded you? Be strong and courageous. Do not be terrified; do not be discouraged, for the Lord your God will be with you wherever you go."

~Joshua 1:9

All the adults who had a part in my upbringing loved me and there were many tender moments for which I will always be grateful, but they also raised me with fear and used anger and disapproval to shame and control me. (I've forgiven them, but secrets and shame hide in darkness while the truth sets us free. It's time to shine light on the truth of what we struggle with so we can get free, heal our wounds, and do better for those who come after us.) My caregivers wanted to protect me from the dangers of the world and ensure I'd always do what a Christian should. (I will always be thankful they introduced me to Jesus, but it was confusing to feel occasional comfort and peace and then be overwhelmed by their anger, and feel afraid, ashamed, and rejected.)

I, too, parented in fear, but I was turned off by religious ideals and spent many years not going to church. Church felt like a place of judgment and rejection. Why would I go someplace I felt more disapproval and shame?! (I didn't know at the time that *relationship* with God is different than *religion* and there's no shame in a relationship with Jesus. Religion is rules made up by people. Relationships are built from the heart, but for many years I couldn't feel anything but a heavy weight of anger, sadness [that I would later recognize as shame], and fear blocking my heart, so all I knew was religion.)

Like my caregivers, I was afraid my kids wouldn't turn out 'the right way' if I didn't do everything perfectly with them or if they didn't always behave appropriately. I was afraid they'd be injured somehow if I didn't aggressively ensure their safety by shouting commands (that were unnecessary to remind them of when they reached a certain age!) such as, "Watch for cars!" Or, "Stay by me in the store!" I was worried others would judge me for my parenting, that they'd disapprove of how I was raising my children. Parenting this way results in anxious, scared, and angry people at risk of repeating the same worry-based cycle with their own kids.

Fear causes us to control and manipulate, thinking we won't be taken care of or that something terrible will happen if we aren't micromanaging every detail. Anything outside of God that we look to for our peace, safety, security, or approval can become an area we try to control and manipulate.

As much as I didn't want to continue this pattern with my children, I'd subconsciously taken on every one of the traits modeled by my caregivers. Before I knew it, I was the scared, angry adult who wasn't taking ownership of my thoughts, emotions, or behavior. I wasn't modeling faith in God. (I believed in God, but *believing in Him* and *putting your faith in Him* are two different things!) I was modeling faith in *my* ability to keep everyone safe and on the 'right path' by using control through fear and anger. For many years, I was unaware that I was repeating the processes I'd witnessed growing up.

(*And* I didn't realize until decades later that I'd also subliminally acquired a tendency to protect abusers from the consequences of their actions. To make excuses for them. To wait out the chaos thinking it would eventually get better. To never hold them accountable or make them apologize when they were wrong. I learned you ignore the angry outbursts, pretend they never happened. Go on as if everything is great, hoping you aren't the target of the next display of emotional violence.)

When I became a parent, more often than not, I felt tense and annoyed, but instead of taking responsibility for what I was feeling, I wanted someone else to fix it or feel it with me. (Because if you can make someone feel responsible for your emotions and behavior, you can control them! In my mind, I *needed* to control my kids to make sure they were safe and turned out 'right.') I acted out my emotions. If I was irritable, my kids were on edge because they didn't want my irritation turned toward them. They were anxious and afraid. Because of my controlling behavior, they began to take on undue responsibility for my happiness.

Subconsciously, I didn't feel peace, safety, or security unless I was in control. Being in control made me feel that I was protecting my kids, but with my words and behavior, I made my children feel *responsible* for me-for my worry and for my anger. I knew no other way to feel peaceful and calm, so I gained a false sense of peace by controlling my environment and the people in it (in this case, my sweet children).

Why do we do this? The root of the problem is that fearful, angry people have been victimized (likely by the fearful, angry people who raised *them*!). We're terrified that if we don't have control of people and circumstances, we (or our loved ones) will be hurt. We become controlling and manipulative because we think that if we're in control of everyone and everything, nothing bad will happen. In our experience, abusers weren't held accountable for their actions-for various reasons-none of which was our responsibility. They never apologized or asked for forgiveness, so we act out our fear, anger, and need for justice.

Even if we're no longer in an abusive situation, *we're trying to heal past hurts in our current relationships-whether we realize it or not!* We want others to feel responsible for us and take care of us because we weren't taken care of in the past when we desperately needed to be. We need to feel in control, so we feel safe.

We're afraid we'll be hurt if we let down our walls of anger.

It looks like we're blaming others for our feelings, but the truth is: someone else *is* to blame for the pain and anger we feel inside. Someone else hurt us. Victimization teaches us that we're not responsible for what happens to us or the feelings that result-because we *were not* responsible! Someone else's actions are the reason for our pain. Our power was taken from us. We didn't have a choice about what took place.

But when we stay stuck in fear, anger, and external control, we're continuing the dysfunctional cycle, and we aren't tapping into our God-given power to experience peace and joy in life.

We need to be gracious, gentle, and compassionate with ourselves as we look at the reasons we think and feel the ways we do. We aren't responsible for causing the fear, pain, and anger we feel inside, but to change and grow, we have to own our power to take responsibility for what we choose to do with our thoughts and feelings moving forward.

Our power was taken from us for a time, but we own this moment right now.

When we look for our peace, safety, and security in our ability to control others, or our circumstances, we're giving away our power because we're relying on something outside ourselves-something outside of God in us-for the lasting peace and joy that only He can give!

While I had been victimized as a child and *other people* were culpable for their actions toward me at the time, *I* was now responsible for my fear, anger, and the controlling behavior I was displaying toward others, but I wasn't taking responsibility.

Until we take ownership of our thoughts, words and actions-claiming our God-given power to make our lives what we want them to be-we seek a false sense of safety by trying to control and manipulate everyone and everything. We need others to feel responsible for our feelings so that we can control them, and so we feel taken care of. Until the injustices that were done to us are addressed, it's impossible to feel responsible for our emotions! We didn't cause the pain and anger inside us. Someone else was the cause. But *we* have to deal with the rage we feel about how we were treated.

It doesn't go away if we ignore it. In other words, we aren't responsible for causing the hurt and anger that we feel, but we are accountable for how we deal with it.

What do I mean by "make our lives what we want them to be"? It means we're not slaves to our emotions-helpless to do anything other than act them out or use our moods to control others. Making my life what I want it to be means I take responsibility for *all* my thoughts and feelings, which is one of the hardest things to do after enduring abuse. It can be infuriating and extremely uncomfortable, but this is how we begin to get our power back.

Our anger and fear because of what we've suffered are justified. Abuse should never happen. Only when our pain is validated and we accept ourselves as we are-without judgment-taking ownership of our thoughts, feelings, and actions, can we move forward.

The path forward isn't always linear. Different people and circumstances bring up issues in us we need to examine. Healing can take many years, especially when we've been wounded as children. We become comfortable with chaos. We find that we have subconsciously chosen people who perpetuate dysfunction in our lives.

We choose people who are codependent, who don't take responsibility for themselves, and we end up becoming overly responsible for them and we want them to be responsible for us! The relationship becomes a back-and-forth dance of control and manipulation. But because we aren't meant to control other people, choosing codependent people to be in relationship with delays us getting to our core issues.

To put it another way, when we've chosen partners, friends, circumstances that require us to think we need to take responsibility for other people's behavior to feel safe, we've put ourselves in a situation that instead of growing and changing, we do what we have always done, and we stay stuck in a pattern of anger, external control, over responsibility for others, and denial of responsibility for ourselves.

How do codependent relationships keep us from taking responsibility for ourselves? The answer is that both parties blame each other for their feelings and actions, but the truth is, they aren't wrong! If I'm in a codependent relationship, the chances are good that the foundation of that relationship is emotional abuse, control, and manipulation. If I'm emotionally abusing someone, I *am* the reason they're angry and scared or sad and defeated. It's impossible to take ownership of our feelings when we're being emotionally abused, because *someone else is the cause*!

We need to be in a safe environment to take responsibility for our feelings because in an abusive relationship, someone else is the reason for what we're feeling. Once we're safe, we can start to heal and realize everyone is accountable for themselves. Our internal and relationship dynamics begin to change when we feel safe enough to say, "I'm responsible for me and you're responsible for you."

Until we realize that no amount of control we attempt to exert over others will provide the peace we're looking for, we can't truly be free. We can't find our power inside ourselves to experience peace and joy in life if we're attempting to control others by being overly responsible for them or by blaming them, trying to make them feel responsible for our moods and actions! The reason we blame others or try to make them feel responsible for us is because we don't know that our worth, value, safety, security, and inner peace come from God-not our ability to control others. Until we realize this, we continue to deny our power to take ownership of ourselves-our thoughts, feelings, and actions-and make our lives what we want them to be.

As a military wife, I was emotionally immature and felt abandoned (and therefore, victimized) because I was raising our children by myself half the time. My husband was home about a year then gone a year-off and on-for twelve years.

I felt sorry for myself and wanted others to see how much I was suffering. I showed my "suffering" in my angry, annoyed moods.

I wanted other people (even my precious children) to feel responsible for me, so they'd take care of me and help me feel better.

(I *hate* that I was like this, but I want others to get free, so I'm telling the truth.)

I wasn't consciously aware of all the ways my fear, anger, control, and manipulation were hurting my children, but I could see the pain on their faces. My mouth was moving, but I wasn't taking time to think about what I was saying, how I was saying it, or how it would affect them. Truthfully, I needed them to be affected by my moods and behavior because it was the only way I felt safe and in control. (I feel deep regret that I was like this, but I didn't know how to change.)

Instead of working to process difficult emotions with an adult friend, I over shared my feelings with my children. I made my adult problems their problems. I didn't want to feel alone in my struggles.

This led my kids to feel responsible for other people. It caused them to look outside themselves for their value and self-worth.

Parenting this way causes our kids' identity to become entangled in the moods and behavior of others. My behavior made them stressed, fearful, and anxious-all the things I didn't want my kids to feel-because I hadn't learned that *I'm responsible for me*. When we parent this way, children begin to think, "If someone is happy, I feel good about myself. If someone is angry, I'm responsible. Something about me has made them angry. Their mood is my fault and I have to fix it. I have to help them feel better. It's who I am."

Parenting this way makes kids feel ashamed and leads to codependency and insecurity. Children miss out on a carefree, happy childhood because they're parenting their parents. While I wanted the best for my children, my words and actions resulted in hurt, scared, and angry people, at risk of repeating the same fear-based cycle. I knew no other way to be.

As time went on, I desperately wanted to change. I had deep remorse and a broken heart for how I was hurting my family, but old habits lingered. My tone of voice had become such that even when I didn't *feel* angry, I *sounded* angry.

Where to start? Life is too precious to go day in and day out and not treasure the people you care most about. This starts with a tender heart. Until we believe that our loved ones are gifts to cherish, our words, and actions toward them won't reflect that. I never wanted to waste a second with my children. Their childhood was a chance for me to give them everything I needed from my parents. But you can't give what you don't have!

I failed many times as a mom, yelling at my children, maintaining control through fear and anger. I floundered because I didn't have the education, skills, or awareness of God's unconditional acceptance of, and love for, me-all of which are needed to manage the tricky stuff that comes up when your sweet, cooing baby becomes a toddler with their own ideas and desires in life! My failures break my heart because I know they broke my kids' hearts.

Time is a gift. Those precious souls you've been given are gifts. The problems come when we don't know how to love ourselves and so cannot love others the way we want to. 1 John 4:18 says, "There is no fear in love. But perfect love drives out fear…." We can only love because God first loved us (see 1 John 4:19).

To learn to love ourselves, we need to believe we are unconditionally approved of and loved by God. Then we must become aware that our peace, safety, and security comes from God's unconditional love for us and not from other people.

We need to deal with the fear and anger we have about how we were mistreated. We need to process our thoughts and feelings, recognizing the beliefs behind our behaviors.

We have to realize we aren't responsible for the moods, words, or actions of anyone but ourselves, and we need to stop living in fear, anger, and control, looking for a false sense of peace and safety in our ability to control others!

Mindsets to Move Forward

Faith in God

There's a difference between *believing in God* and *putting our faith and trust in Him.*

I understand the fear and concern that come with letting go of control and manipulation. When we live in fear and terrible things have happened in our lives, we hold on tightly to control. We're angry we were hurt and we're afraid we'll be hurt again. We need to feel that we're doing something to protect ourselves and our loved ones. Even when our control measures make people angry and afraid, we feel protected when we control.

We don't feel we're doing enough if we aren't controlling. We don't feel that we're safe if we aren't manipulating people and situations to go the way we think they should, but the truth is, we've never been in control.

God decides what happens on Earth!

Faith in God doesn't mean we never face difficult times in life. Faith in God means that in the midst of our trials, we have a peace that passes our human understanding (see Philippians 4:7). Our hope in God anchors our souls (see Hebrews 6:19). When we put our trust in Jesus, He is our Firm Foundation, the Rock we stand on to get us through our troubles (see Matthew 8:24-27).

Letting go of control doesn't make sense to our human minds, especially when we've faced so much pain, but God promises we can trust in Him. When we believe in His promises, we activate our faith and supernatural peace and hope take root in our hearts! I pray we come to know that our hearts are safe only in Our Creator's hands. We humans do our best to love, but NO ONE CAN LOVE YOU LIKE JESUS!

Get The Chaos Out of Conversation

A key role for parents is to help our children learn to put their feelings into words so they don't act them out. Don't yell at your children, then tell them not to yell when they're angry. They will absorb like sponges everything they see us do and everything they hear us say.

There is a saying, "More is caught than is taught." In other words, even when we don't speak, we're sending messages. Children learn from our behavior. Some parents will argue, "My children should do what I *say* and not what they *see* me do." This is neither logical nor practical. Our words and behavior become their words and behavior, and ultimately, what they believe about themselves.

Don't interrupt when others are speaking. Write down your questions or comments if necessary. Take a deep breath. Practice self-control and wait your turn. If you start to interrupt, apologize, and allow the other person to continue. (My husband knows I've struggled with this, but I'm getting better!)

If someone interrupts you, immediately stop talking until they stop talking, then finish what you started saying. This is a nonverbal way of helping others learn to wait their turn.

Take responsibility for all your emotions. Your emotions aren't for someone else to fix and make you feel better. Stop trying to feel a sense of power by how much control you can exert over others. As long as we act like someone else is responsible for us, we leave ourselves powerless and unchanged.

The second we take responsibility, it can feel awkward, uncomfortable, foreign. It's a hit to our pride. We may feel alone and vulnerable.

People may be angry with us for our previous behavior, and if we've used fear to control and manipulate them, they should be!

When our loved ones start to feel safe, they'll have emotions they need to process-feelings they weren't safe to assess before. Be patient. These precious people have been anxious and afraid for too long and need to know you can be trusted. They'll test your authenticity. They may say, "We'll see how long this will last," or, "Aren't you going to yell?"

It's a long road to healing and sometimes children who've been raised in an angry environment don't truly begin to heal until they're out of that atmosphere-even if you have changed.

We may feel bright and happy, but if in the past, your family never knew when you'd explode in anger, they don't trust the happy mood. We have to be authentically changed in our hearts and earn their trust. This takes time.

If we're truly remorseful, we'll allow them the space they need to reestablish a connection with themselves that they didn't have the freedom to have while they were under our control. Continue to pursue positive changes, and pray they get free and don't repeat the cycle of codependency, based in fear, anger, control, and intimidation in their own relationships.

Heart changes can be very difficult to implement into your everyday life. We may find ourselves quickly slipping back into old habits-condescending tones of voice, angry attitudes, sarcasm. When this happens, say, "I apologize. My tone wasn't what I wanted it to be just then. I'm working on it."

Find someone whose tone of voice reflects how you'd like to sound. Mimic the tone. It will feel weird and fake in the beginning (because our tone of voice reflects our habitual thought patterns, and habits take time to change)! Your family may look at you strangely and you may sense their walls going up because it's normal to resist transitions at first.

Talk to them. Acknowledge when you don't sound the way you want to. Tell them you know your tone, at times, *sounds* angry even when you don't *feel* angry, and you want to change it. Apologize and keep working to get better. Change doesn't just happen. It takes effort. We have to practice a new tone of voice, a new reaction other than anger.

*Use an app or website to practice matching the sound of musical notes.

*Hum and feel the vibration of the different notes in your chest. In fact, according to Peiting Lien (2021), Doctor of Physical Therapy, humming helps heal the nervous system and aids in oxygen delivery throughout the body![1]

*Listen to music that makes you happy.

*Take time to be quiet and meditate. Spend time in God's presence and in His Word every day. When I do this first thing in the morning, my day goes more smoothly. He is my Rock and Foundation (Luke 6:46-47). I need to spend time alone with Him to fill up my spirit before I start to engage in conversation with others. For moms or caregivers, I know this can feel almost impossible, but start somewhere. Have quiet time when your children nap. This space set aside to feed your spirit heals you and gives you the strength to be the best you can be for your sweet children.

God can make up for the time your family lost because of your anger. I know that, quite often, my moods and behavior were not pleasant to be around. We had a lot of good times, but I have many regrets.

My purpose is to tell the truth to help others heal. I want you and your family to experience freedom from unhealthy behavior.

*Don't underestimate the power of therapy! I consider myself very self-aware, but when I started seeing a therapist, she brought things to my attention that I didn't notice on my own! When you recognize changes you'd like to make, consider finding a counselor who can assist you in getting to the roots of your beliefs about yourself that are driving your behavior. It shows courage and self-awareness to seek help in improving ourselves and our relationships. A heart that is healing is a light for others!

Chapter 5

The Start of Change

In Thessalonians 5:16, Paul tells the church, "Be joyful always." But what if we don't feel joyful, and are rarely even happy? What if, instead, we're angry, sad, tired, scared, confused? If you've read this verse and want to be joyful but cannot work out how exactly that's supposed to happen, I want to encourage you. When we've been burdened with hurts, fear, anger, sadness, shame, guilt, and aren't certain how to unpack those feelings, "be joyful always" feels impossible!

Here's the key: We cannot get to a place where we have joy in our spirits regardless of our circumstances until we understand what's taken place in our lives that has kept our hearts blocked.

Additionally, we need to feel safe before we can get to the core of our hearts. I'm not going to take that the shield off my heart if I know that in so doing, I'll immediately be hurt again. It's crucial to have relationships with safe people whose interest is our healing-people who want to see us go higher in life-people who don't judge us for what we've done or what we've been through-people who understand the reasons for our behaviors and who believe we're worthy of love and acceptance as we are.

This doesn't mean finding people who allow you to behave any way you want to! The best relationships are those in which each person takes responsibility for their behavior and points out (in love!) when we're not taking responsibility for ourselves! A good friend might say, "It seems to me that you're blaming others/this situation for your actions." Then, (because we're growing and changing!), we say, "Thank you for bringing that to my attention. I'll look at what thoughts and feelings are driving my behavior." (Of course, we're *never* offended when our friends offer gentle guidance!)

To start dismantling the walls over our hearts, we must admit our true feelings. Why? Because what we resist persists. What do I mean by that? It means that if I know I'm angry and I feel angry, but I force a smile, stuff my feelings, pretend everything is fine, I'll never get to the reason for my anger.

There've been times I was embarrassed to admit (even to myself!) that certain things made me angry. But after sitting with my thoughts and assessing the cause of my anger, I was empowered with self-awareness. Knowing the *reason* I was affected helped me take responsibility for my feelings and enabled me to manage my emotions with more logic.

What does it mean to manage our emotions with logic? It means that just because we *feel* an emotion doesn't mean we have to *act* on it!

You may think, "How can I feel something and not act on it?" I understand that concern! I've boiled over with anger on the inside and felt that the only way to get relief from the intense feeling was to *act* it out. Usually, I yelled. Often, I slammed things. Once I threw a glass candle. I'm not proud of my actions. In fact, my heart is convicted at the memory of them. I relate them to you to convey that I deeply understand the struggle for self-control.

To answer the question, a change occurs when we see that our actions are hurting others. My heart was broken by the way I hurt my loved ones. I knew I didn't want to continue in that vein, so I decided that when I felt overwhelming anger, I would do something different. I started to *say*, "I'm feeling angry." I started to *talk* about my emotions instead of acting them out.

Mindsets to Move Forward

Our hearts become hardened when we're raised in fear and anger and when we continue the cycle of control in our adult lives. I started to change when my heart was broken by the sadness and fear on my kids' faces. Until our hearts break with the things that break God's heart, we don't change. Pray that God will take your heart of stone and give you a heart of flesh (see Ezekiel 11:19).

Don't be ashamed of any of your feelings, but don't act out your feelings. Because we learn by repetition: Do not slam or throw things to show people that you're angry. This serves only to create fear in your family members. You have a choice: let the cycle of pain, hell, and chaos continue or consciously make the decision to choose a different reaction.

When we talk it out instead of acting it out, we're taking responsibility for ourselves.

Many of us who've come from fearful, angry, controlling backgrounds may quickly shut down a sensation of joy because it feels foreign. It can feel like we're letting our guards down. If our guards are down, we're not in control and our experience in life has been that if we're not in control, we get hurt. Joy, peace, and feeling freedom to laugh in life feels scary. When we start to change, we might notice that the emotion of joy makes us feel vulnerable and awkward. This is the reason it's vital to renew our minds daily with God's Word.

Declaring God's Word

Psalm 139:14 says, "I praise you because I am fearfully and wonderfully made; your works are wonderful…."

You are one of the works of God. That means, *you* are wonderful! Try saying that out loud!

*"I am wonderful!"

*"I am wonderful!"

*"I am wonderful!"

Say it until you believe it and feel life-giving joy flood your heart! I can't help but smile when I say this. Why? "Pleasant words are a honeycomb, sweet to the soul and healing to the bones," Psalm 16:24!

We honor God when we love ourselves because He loves us!

In Isaiah 54:10, God tells Isaiah, "Though the mountains be shaken and the hills be removed, yet my *unfailing love* [emphasis added] for you will not be shaken…."

*THE CREATOR OF THE UNIVERSE LOVES ME!

*I am lovable.

Nehemiah 8:10 says, "…the joy of the Lord is your strength"!

*There is joy in my heart. This isn't a lie. There is joy underneath the hurt and anger. We just have to do some digging!

*I think positive thoughts about myself on purpose!

Be proactive in your thought life. Take a stand against the voices of guilt and shame that we sometimes find in our heads. When these thoughts creep in, try saying, “STOP! I will not listen to lies! God loves me, approves of me, and I am wonderful!”

BE BOLD. Let the lion in your heart roar with hope that you can have peace and happiness in life. Take a deep breath. Every bit of work you do counts. Every time you’re honest with yourself about your thoughts and feelings, every time you take responsibility for your emotions, words, and actions, and every time you choose a healthy response to anger, you move in the direction of a more peaceful, joyful life.

Keep loving yourself. Keep taking responsibility. Keep reading your Bible. Keep seeking God.

Chapter 6

*Chipping Away at The Fear of Man**

*Genesis 1:27 indicates that "man" means males and females (i.e., all hu-mans).

One of the most beautiful things about healing from fear of others and knowing what we are and are not responsible for, is that our inner peace has the potential to create an atmosphere that allows others the freedom to be true to themselves and find their own inner peace and healing.

If our energy has been constantly externally focused to ensure our emotional or physical safety, we haven't had the psychological space to assess what's going on inside ourselves. Living in fear causes our hearts to become numb because it isn't safe to let our guards down. Our hearts become hardened to protect us from further harm.

Emotional safety would have allowed us the freedom to observe our personal thoughts and feelings. But because of fear, we've never had the opportunity to get to know who we are.

When we get out of an emotionally abusive environment, and start to feel safe, all the thoughts and feelings we were either too afraid to have, or didn't have the psychological space to explore, start to surface. If we don't deal with our feelings from being raised in-or experiencing-a controlling, angry environment, we risk repeating harmful habits in our relationships with our children and others.

Once we're safe, it's normal to feel angry, confused, sad, hurt, irritated, frustrated, lost. It's normal to be concerned about what people are thinking of us because in the past, in an abusive environment, people *were* watching us and judging us negatively. We were made to believe that our identity-our worth and value-is tied to other people's opinions of us. We were made to feel that if someone was angry, it was because of something we did or didn't do. We've learned to feel overly responsible for the moods, words, and actions of other people.

When we've learned to look outside ourselves for acceptance, validation, and assurance of our worth, people sense that we need their approval, and we're vulnerable to being controlled and manipulated. We're afraid of not being liked and accepted. In short, we're afraid of what others think of us.

Proverbs 29:25 says, "Fear of man will prove to be a snare…," but how do we stop being afraid of what others think of us, afraid we won't be liked, accepted, approved, validated, loved?

To begin, we realize we don't need approval or acceptance from every human we meet because Our Creator, the King of kings and Lord of lords, loves us, and accepts us-exactly as we are, today, right here in this moment-regardless of what we've ever said or done-at any time in our lives-and regardless of what has ever been said or done to us. *We are unconditionally loved by God.*

When we know God loves us and accepts us, we're empowered to stop fearing whether people approve of us. No longer afraid, we're not susceptible to *being* controlled or *to* control.

Free from the fear of man, we can hear clearly from Our Creator, and have the courage to do what He prompts us to do. Why? We're no longer slaves to what others think of us and therefore, we cannot be controlled by their rejection-or by their acceptance! Empowered from within by God's acceptance and love, we have the fortitude to act as He urges us instead of ignoring His voice and doing something to look cool in front of our peers!

This is what Jesus meant when He said in Matthew 12:50, "For whoever does the will of my Father in heaven is my brother and sister and mother."

Once we realize we don't need every human on Earth to like us and approve of us, we stop feeling rejected and ashamed when we don't get someone's approval. We don't need it!

When we get to know God, we learn to love and accept ourselves right where we are because God loves us and accepts us as we are (see John 3:16). Only when we believe this can we feel safe. Once we feel safe, we can start to be honest about what's in our hearts and begin to heal. God loves us with an unconditional love-a perfect love that drives out fear (see 1 John 4:18). Your heart is safe in your Creator's hands. Romans 10:11 says, "Anyone who trusts in him will never be put to shame."

You can trust God with what's in your heart. He already knows anyway!

Mindsets to Move Forward

1. Stop caring what other people think of you. In other words, stop trying to get approval from every person you meet.
2. See if you can think of specific words or behaviors from your caregivers that you sent you wrong messages about yourself. For example, did one parent get up and leave the table every time you joined the group? Were you overly criticized or drastically punished for minor things? Did one parent seem disappointed in you no matter what you did? Did you get the

message you weren't good enough or you weren't what they wanted in a child?

3. Recognize that all those behaviors were wrong, hurtful, and sinful, and you never should have been treated like that. Your hurt, anger, and sadness are valid. It hurts deeply to be rejected by a parent. But know that their behavior has *nothing* to do with you. People who treat children in those ways don't love and accept themselves and don't have love and acceptance to give.
4. Replace lies that you're not worthy or valuable with truths from God's Word.
5. What your Creator says about you supersedes *anything and everything* anyone else has ever said about you-good or bad!
6. Don't look for your peace in the words or behaviors of another human. Humans aren't perfect. Your peace can be found only in your relationship with Your Creator.
7. People can tell us all day that God loves us, but if we haven't had His love modeled to us, it can be very hard to believe. There are churches filled with people who will accept you and not judge you, showing you God's love-and will also tell you the truth-that you need to do your part! You need to renew your mind daily, keep seeking Him in His Word. Keep going to church. When you seek Him, you *will* find Him.

8. We cannot get filled up with man's approval of us. Putting our trust in other humans is not a firm foundation. Humans are flawed, imperfect. We cannot be what other people need from us all the time. Only God, Our Creator, can meet our every need according to His riches in glory (see Philippians 4:19). In other words, we can trust Him to fill our hearts with His Holy Spirit, His peace, and His presence.
9. Don't feel like you have to have all the answers to move forward. When we praise God in faith, He moves for us and changes things in us that we, in our human efforts, could never change.

Jesus told his disciples in Luke 24:49, "...stay in the city until you have been clothed with power from on high." For some of us, there's a season when we're meant to have a lot of time to ourselves-time to assess what's in our hearts and to process and reflect on what has taken place in our lives. Time to fortify our city walls. Until we know the reasons, or the beliefs, that drive the emotions that come up in us, and until we realize that our worth and value is not found in other people's acceptance or approval of us, we cannot know how to heal and move forward.

Right now, you may not like people. People may get on your nerves. You may crave all the time to yourself you can possibly get. I understand. People have hurt you. People can be annoying and unsafe. But one day, when your heart has healed more and you begin to love yourself and see yourself the way God sees you, you'll know that life is a gift. You'll smile when you see someone else's heart touched. Your heart will crave to do good for others.

You'll feel gratitude and warmth you never felt before that moment. Hold on. Keep listening to your heart-even if there are several angry layers to work through! Ask yourself why you feel the way you do. Keep hoping and keep going!

Always Remember:

**You are unconditionally loved, accepted, and approved of by The Creator of the Universe! Period!*

**There is no shame on you-NO MATTER WHAT!*

**Isaiah 54:17 says, "...Every tongue that accuses you in judgment, you will condemn." Condemn means to disapprove of.[1] In other words, don't approve of the judgments others make of you!*

Only what your Creator says about you is valid!

Romans 8:1 says, "Therefore, there is now no condemnation for those who are in Christ Jesus." In Christ Jesus, we are not disapproved of, WE ARE ACCEPTED.

**Every breath is a new beginning. With each breath, remind yourself, I am loved EXACTLY as I am.*

**God made you for a purpose and His purpose for you will prevail! (Proverbs 19:21)*

Chapter 7

Turning Inward

Because God lives in us, to overcome the need for external validation, and the belief that we need to control and manipulate people and circumstances to feel peaceful, safe, and secure, we must turn inward. In Luke 17:21, Jesus tells us, "…the kingdom of God is within you," and in Matthew 6:33, Jesus says, "But seek first his kingdom and his righteousness, and all these other things will be given to you as well."

An external focus is one of the greatest thieves of peace. Unfortunately, if we've been accustomed to an environment in which we haven't had a sense of well-being because our physical or emotional safety, and our self-perception depended on what mood others were in, we've been robbed of the psychological space to feel calm and quiet and look inward. We've been externally focused to protect ourselves and haven't had the chance to experience the beauty and stillness that resides inside of us. We've learned that our peace, safety, value, and worth is altogether dependent upon other people's words and actions.

For us, the idea that the kingdom of God-a kingdom of unconditional love, peace, safety, and security-is inside of us can feel foreign and almost wrong.

But the truth is God lives in every one of us. Just as children share DNA with their parents, The Creator of the Universe is in His creation. God is all and is in all (see Ephesians 4:6). It's His breath in our lungs (see Genesis 2:7). His light is our light (see John 1:9). His peace is our peace (see Isaiah 26:12).

My Experience with Yoga

Psalm 46:10 says, "Be still and know that I am God…." One of the first ways I learned to be still and feel inner peace was by practicing yoga-yoga as an exercise science, not as a religion. The reason I make this distinction is because there are varying opinions among followers of Jesus Christ regarding whether Christians should practice yoga.

For example, when I first became a certified yoga teacher, I called a Catholic church and asked the priest if I could teach there. He told me that the Catholic Church does not participate in activities in which people could become possessed. In my mind, I thought, "What, now?!" He was pleasant about it, but I was surprised he felt that way.

I thanked him for his time and discussed his response with a yoga teacher who was mentoring me. She said she'd never heard of such a thing and that she herself was Catholic!

Two Christians with two different opinions about a topic. It's okay! It happens. It doesn't mean the priest was right and I was wrong or vise verse.

God made our brains and bodies. Yoga is a gift. Just as someone with low sugar in their blood is anxious and literally starving for what they need, so too had my soul been deprived of peace and stillness. Having known mainly internal chaos, practicing yoga helped regulate my brain and body, putting me on a path toward less anxiety and more rational thinking. By calming my over-anxious mind, I became more aware of the presence of God in me. I became aware of His peace!

Knowing the benefits I'd experienced from my practice, I was excited to share them with others. I eventually was given permission to teach at an elementary school. I also taught adults on an Army base.

Scientific evidence abounds detailing the advantages of yoga, such as, lowered blood pressure, better sleep quality, ability to quickly recover from stress.[1] Yoga is a tool God has given us to improve our lives on Earth. Just as medications can regulate our brains and bodies, yoga does the same. It's an ideal practice for people who have experienced trauma.

How do I know? Until I discovered yoga, my body was wrought with physical tension-tight jaw, tight lower back, tight solar plexus (I've found that some doctors don't like the term "solar plexus," which I find annoying, but it's the "upper gastric region" or upper part of your abdomen below your breastbone.) Inside, I was filled with fear, anxiety, and a not-so-healthy amount of explosive rage.

Case in point: When my husband and I were first seeing each other, he and I were sitting in his room in our Army barracks talking when another woman came to the door. Thinking it would be awkward if I stayed while she visited him, I left but I wasn't happy about it! (This was before I'd developed much confidence or assertive communication. And I certainly had zero skills in pressing into uncomfortable feelings!)

In lieu of saying anything in the moment, I avoided my feelings until I closed the door to my room and proceeded to have a breakdown in which I yelled and threw things. (This is what happens when God isn't in your relationship!) Instead of being able to trust the Holy Spirit in him (because neither he nor I had a personal relationship with Jesus at the time), I felt *I* had to be the one to control him and make sure he did the right thing. The only way I knew to control any situation was to become angry and make sure the other person knew it.

His room was right next to mine in the barracks, so he knew it! The woman didn't stay long. After a minute or so of my quite-loud outburst, my future husband knocked on my door and I let him in. I was in tears of rage and fear because I'd seen this other woman as a threat to our relationship. He held me until I calmed down and we went tentatively along with our dating life-both of us scared to be alone, so we tolerated each other's dysfunction. He put up with a lot from me and I put up with a lot from him! But he's been gracious and forgiving and has loved me in a way I never knew before. His love helped my heart heal and I can honestly say I don't know where I'd be today if I hadn't had him in my life.

As you will read in Chapter 23, I know that lasting peace-peace that passes understanding-comes when we give our hearts to Jesus and God sends us His Holy Spirit, but yoga is one of the avenues that God used for me to begin to heal and find stillness. When you practice stillness, it's easier to get back to that place when you need it. Before yoga, my mind was busy, and my body was tense. I was reading my Bible and attending church, but I needed a practical approach that could impact change on a physiological level. As discussed in Chapter 2, our brains and bodies need to be regulated.

The practice of yoga calmed my mind, which facilitated the transition from emotional reactivity to logic and critical thinking. With a more relaxed, detached position, I was able to begin processing the thoughts and feelings that had shaped my self-perception and worldview. Through yoga, I disciplined my mind and body, bringing my human nature under more conscious control. The practice laid the foundation for me to begin to differentiate between a human controlling response and the guidance of The Holy Spirit, which often feels like a peaceful urgency to act or speak.

The translation of the word *yoga* from Sanskrit means *union.*[2] The practice brings together body with mind, breath with movement. It's an active stillness that works to regulate an overactive stress response. The fight, flight, or freeze system is brought back under more conscious control. Active stillness means you feel the physical challenge of a pose, but your breath and your mind are quiet and serene. You're able to be fully present, but *detached* from the stress of the moment, meaning you're not trying to control the moment, you're *observing* it, which translates to more calm, focused, and detached awareness in the face of stressors off the mat.

With my brain and body in a calmer state, I became more *self-aware*, which is paramount in healing from trauma. I began to make note of what happened in my body when certain thoughts and feelings surfaced. I was able to observe the physical sensation and trace the thoughts behind it. Mind/body awareness helped me realize when and where I was holding tension. Chronic tension leads to blocked energy, which can make us sick. Yoga taught me to stretch and breathe into tight areas, releasing blockages. (See Chapter 14 for more on how emotions and chronic tension affect our bodies.)

In the Army, I was doing PT (physical training) at least five days a week-pushups, sit ups, two-mile (or six-mile-whatever the leader wanted that day!) runs-but no form of exercise worked to regulate my body and mind the way yoga does. Yoga teaches mindfulness-being present and observing your thoughts and feelings in the moment without trying to change them.

Prior to discovering yoga, I was in the habit of avoiding my feelings and trying to control each moment to feel safe. Yoga provided a foundation for me to overcome my resistance to feeling uncomfortable emotions and get in touch with my heart. By observing my emotions and remaining detached from them (noticing them without trying to change them), I learned a more peaceful way of responding to my thoughts and feelings in everyday life.

Nothing but your relationship with Jesus Christ will bring you lasting peace, but God has given us tools to improve our lives on Earth and yoga is one of them.

Mindsets to Move Forward

To begin to cultivate inner awareness, see if you can notice where in your body you feel various emotions. When I've experienced anxiety about what people were thinking of me, I've felt tension in my temples and my jaw clenches. I start to hold my breath and my heart rate increases. If you find yourself worried about the judgments of others, release the breath you're likely holding (!), then take a deep breath, and remember that you're unconditionally loved, approved of, and accepted by Your Creator.

While we cannot control what others are thinking, we can empower ourselves by developing a habit of healthy detachment from external validation. As with yoga, we can be fully present, but unaffected by the stress of the moment. We can notice the challenging sensation of fear of judgement or desire for approval, but we maintain an inner stillness that separates us from the anxiety and the need to act on it.

With practice, we develop inner calm and stillness that result from mindfulness (observing the moment without trying to change it). When your mind suggests you go back to an old way of thinking (fear of negative judgement or needing external approval), you have the power to make a different choice. You are peacefully detangled from the effects of other's thoughts, words, and actions. You realize, "I'm responsible for me, and you're responsible for you."

There are days I feel vulnerable and am more easily thrown off my center. There are days I'm tired or not feeling my best and am affected more than I want to be by people's behaviors or my desire for acceptance. But I can always take a minute to recognize what's happening in my mind and body, close my eyes and feel God's kingdom within me-His peace, His unconditional love, and acceptance and remind myself who I am. 1 Corinthians 15:10 says, "But by the grace of God I am what I am…." I am who I am because of *whose* I am.

I am what God-*My Creator, My Defender, My Father* says I am. If I believe I need the acceptance and approval of other humans to feel inner peace, safety, and security, I don't know the truth of who I am.

It's a *practice* to remind ourselves what God says about us-to renew our minds (see Romans 12:2)-and learn more about who He is every day. The more we know about Him, the more we know about ourselves because when we give our hearts to Jesus, everything He is, God gives to us (see Galatians 4:1-7)! He is our strength, our song, and our salvation (Psalm 118:14)!

If you want to learn more about Him, seek Him. Hebrews 11:6 says, "…God…rewards those who earnestly seek Him." Read His Word. Go to a church that preaches from the Bible and that makes you feel welcomed. They do exist! And very importantly, make quiet time in His presence part of your daily routine. Ecclesiastes 5:2 says, “God is in heaven and you are on earth, so let your words be few.” Listen to Him. Meditate on His Word.

It's exhausting to be constantly externally focused seeking our value and worth in other people’s words and actions, but your self-worth and value comes from Your Creator, not from hypercritical humans! Be internally focused. God is for you.

Mind-Body Awareness

Notice anywhere you’re holding tension in your body and breathe into those places. Common areas we hold tension are our jaws, necks, shoulders, lower backs, and hamstrings (or the upper back of the legs). If you want to, try the following:

*Notice if you’re clenching your teeth together during the day and consciously relax your lower jaw away from your upper jaw. With your lips together, allow your lower teeth to be separate from your upper teeth.

*Sit up straight and relax your shoulders away from your ears, rolling them back and down.

*Sit in a chair with your back straight and your hands on each side of your rib cage. Take a deep breath in through your nose and see if you can feel your ribs expanding into your hands. Exhale through your mouth or your nose. Repeat a few times.

*Sit on the floor with your legs in the shape of the letter "V." Keep your back straight and knees bent to your comfort level as you lean forward to feel a stretch in your legs. Be aware of your breath and whether you're holding tension in other places. If you find tension, consciously release it before continuing. Notice how the stretch changes if you make your "V" wider or narrower. Sitting on a folded blanket or pillow helps keep your back straight. This stretch relieves lower back tension.

*Throughout the day, continue to check in with yourself to see where you're holding tension and consciously relax those areas telling yourself:

"*I am unconditionally loved by The Creator of the Universe.*"

THANK YOU, JESUS!

Chapter 8

Setting Boundaries & Other Bold Words

May we desire God's approval more than we desire approval from man.

Having come from an environment in which I was made to feel responsible for other people's moods and behaviors and feeling that my identity was based therein, I had no idea what it meant to have boundaries in a relationship. By definition, a boundary is a line that marks the limits of an area; a line of a subject or sphere of activity.[1]

The nature of codependency is that you don't know the line where you end, and another person begins. There are no boundaries. There isn't mutual respect. There's control and manipulation because each party wants the other to be responsible for them. Each party looks to the other for validation of their self-worth. For example, let's say Person A feels valid and has a sense of self-worth when they can control Person B who is a people pleaser. Person B feels valid and worthy when they get acceptance and approval for going along with Person A's wishes!

Healthy boundaries in relationships means each person is accountable for themselves and respect is reciprocated. You learn how to be supportive of a person without solving their problems for them. You don't make them feel responsible for your well-being and vice versa. The boundary in the relationship is: "I am responsible for me (my thoughts, words, and actions), and you are responsible for yours."

Boundaries begin in our minds with what we think about ourselves. If we think we're not worthy of love and acceptance without external approval and validation from others-or if we don't feel safe, secure, and at peace unless we are controlling others-our words, actions, and body language will communicate that. People who need external validation attract each other-one as the controller, and one as the people pleaser. (Each person may play the role of the other at any time in the tango of control and manipulation.)

When we're externally focused on others for our self-worth, we're letting our spiritual guards down. We tend to let anyone have a say in our lives when we want approval from them. This can be dangerous in that we ignore our instincts because we value someone's approval over whether they're a safe person to be in a relationship with.

Proverbs 4:23 says, "Above all else guard your heart, for it is the wellspring of life…." When our hearts and minds are focused on the fact that we have God's approval and love, we're not concerned with getting approval from other people. In seeking God and finding our self-worth in Him, our hearts stay protected.

Isaiah 26:3 says, "You will keep in perfect peace him whose mind is steadfast, because he trusts in you." I like what the King James Version (KJV) says, "You will keep him in perfect peace who mind is *stayed* [emphasis added] on you…."

When I was afraid people were judging me negatively and I wanted acceptance and approval from every person I encountered, I didn't have boundaries in relationships!

Craving external validation, I felt I had to move when the other person moved. If they wanted me to go somewhere, I went. I didn't know who I was if I didn't have their approval. I felt rejected and ashamed if someone didn't like me because I thought it meant there was something wrong with me. I allowed myself to be controlled by fear that I would lose people's validation if I had a different opinion than theirs or if I didn't say "Yes" to their every request.

I found my self-worth and identity in the opinions of others. Because I wanted (felt I *needed*) everyone to like me, I was quick to give myself away. In other words, I was quick to base my words and actions on what I thought would make the other person like me. I often set aside my own thoughts and feelings to get approval.

The anxiety I felt when interacting with people made me speed through conversations, not make eye contact, laugh at jokes I didn't take time to think about to determine if they were truly funny. When someone used humor to get *my* approval, my laugh was a sign to them that they had my acceptance, and of course I expected theirs in return!

I allowed myself to be easily controlled and manipulated. I would smile when I didn't feel like it to try to keep people from thinking I was angry or saying my face looked "mean."

There's a double standard for girls and women concerning facial expressions (and other socially influenced "allowable" gender traits) that I find very annoying because it affects our self-perception and can be stifling. Even worse, this double standard and limited thinking regarding acceptable gender characteristics can prevent us getting messages from God. (For more on this topic, see Chapter10.)

We've been socially programmed to think it's normal for a man to have a serious look on his face, to be firm and assertive, but we shame girls and women who display those attributes. Why? We subliminally believe that only men are leaders, and only men can hold positions of authority, while women are meant to follow them.

A woman who shows leadership traits is called an ugly word, told she's angry, condescended, ridiculed-all in an attempt to "put her in her place"-a place society is comfortable with her being-timid, submissive, no thoughts or ideas of her own, all her attention on the men in charge. Women who show leadership traits cannot be controlled and this scares some people.

When I was growing up, girls were encouraged to be nice, polite, quiet, weak, dependent. We were taught these are the characteristics that would win us the acceptance and approval of society. We all want to feel part of our social group, and none of us wants to be given a derogatory label, but because of the social expectations of girls and women, there were times that I ignored my instincts. I smiled to keep the peace because I was conditioned to think it's rude to be assertive. There were times I set aside my uneasiness when I didn't feel safe with someone because I didn't want to be judged a social outcast.

I've been in unsafe scenarios and was too scared to speak up or do anything for fear of what people might think of me. I valued other people's approval over my instincts. If you can relate to this, there is no shame on you! We are *not* responsible for other people's actions! When we realize we don't need acceptance and approval from people, we can *unapologetically*-without explanation-act when our inner voice warns us that something isn't right.

Anger can be a signal that we need to set a boundary. We may not yet know how to put our needs into words, but our anger makes us aware that something is amiss.

When I first started setting boundaries with people, it came from a place of anger and irritation. For over twenty years, I'd looked to others to validate my self-worth, so when I stopped needing everyone's approval, I saw opportunities everywhere to set boundaries! I began in anger and my methods were excessively harsh. (I was tired of feeling taken advantage of and not being taken seriously. I didn't want to leave any room for misinterpretation of my position!) Eventually I realized I can be gentle and humble while being firm, no nonsense, and unyielding.

Building Confidence with Boundaries

In Your Mind

When we don't know our worth, we look for it in the acceptance and approval of other people. Because boundaries start in your mind-with what you think about yourself, once you know you're unconditionally loved, *and are part of*, The Creator of The Universe, your perspective changes. You know that you have worth and value regardless of who approves of you and who does not, no matter what's happened in your life, no matter what anyone has ever said or done, and no matter what you've ever said or done. You hold your shoulders back and lift your head up. You become aware that you have just as much right to be on this planet and take up space as every other person here-man, woman, or child. Your skin color, hair color, and eye color were *divinely orchestrated* by God. People may judge those things negatively saying one is better than another, but when you have a firm foundation in God's Word, you know better. You know you are fearfully and wonderfully made (see Psalm 139:14). You know you are loved and accepted *exactly* as you are. You are God's Creation. We start to build our confidence in setting boundaries when we stop caring so much for the approval of other people and realize we're valid, worthy, loved, and accepted because we were made by *The Creator of The Universe*.

In Your Workplace

Know the policies of the company at which you work and adhere to them. This gives you a stable foundation from which to base your decisions. In doing this, when someone asks you the reason for what you did, you can say, "That's the company policy."

When unsure what to do in a particular situation, consult the written procedure or ask the person in charge for guidance. Hopefully, the person in charge is willing to help. If not, go to the next supervisor.

Working this way can build your confidence by establishing a solid base for your actions.

Additional ways to build self-assurance are by doing what you say you're going to do and telling the truth. We aren't jumpy and anxious we're going to get reprimanded or caught when we know we're doing the right thing!

Following policies and being honest (even when we make a mistake) helps us combat the unfortunate mindset some of us have developed in an abusive environment. In an emotionally unsafe atmosphere, we begin to think that we can't do anything right-that our every word and action will be subjected to scrutiny and found to be lacking.

Coming from that background, our self-assurance is low, and we're constantly fearful of saying or doing the wrong thing.

I found it protective and stabilizing to know the policies and procedures of my workplace, to be honest about what I did not know, and when I made a mistake.

When I was a teenager, I babysat my younger cousins on occasion. One of these times, I accidentally spilled my aunt's perfume on one of the kid's comforters. I was prepared that she'd be angry. When she got home, I told her what happened and instead of anger or even frustration, she said, "Thank you for telling me. The bedding probably needs to be washed anyway." (I was pleasantly surprised by her response because I was expecting angry words!) Having been rewarded for telling the truth, this experience has had an enormous, positive impact on my life.

Assigned Duties

Adhering to assigned duties is important when learning boundaries because each person is responsible for *their* tasks and not *overly* responsible for anyone else's. (Those of us who've struggled with codependency tend to take ownership of jobs that belong to someone else. We do for them what they should be doing for themselves. We volunteer our time and talents to be exploited then we get burned out and resentful and don't understand why!)

In family life assigned duties means allocating chores to each family member. At work it means knowing your job description and working within the boundaries of what you were hired to do.

When I was in the Army, deployed to Bosnia, one of my female sergeants frequently asked me to pick up her clothes from the laundry tent. This obviously wasn't part of my duties as a soldier, and some other sergeants in my platoon told me she was taking advantage of me, but I was scared to tell her "No"! (Which is why she knew she could take advantage!)

I didn't want her to speak ill of me to her sergeant friends or treat me poorly. I wanted approval, so I allowed her to leverage her position over me.

On the last occasion that I went to pick up her clothes, I arrived where the laundry tent was supposed to be and was told it had *burned down* the night before–*with her clothes in it*! I laughed to myself all the way back to our tent! I was even more delighted to hand her laundry ticket back to her and relay the news!

The point is, know what are–and are not–your assigned duties and don't be afraid of not getting approval from your superiors if you say "No" with good reason. This sergeant had no ground to stand on if she were to retaliate or try to punish me for not picking up her laundry!

Don't think that people don't see the favor of God on your life. The right people will have the right perception of you.

God has the final say about your reputation, your promotions at work, and in your change of jobs when necessary. Have a good attitude and do the right thing, but don't allow yourself to be taken advantage of because you need acceptance and approval from humans more than you need it from God.

Assertive Communication

For many years, I had a problem with people not respecting me, not taking me seriously. I was confounded by this. It seemed that if I was pleasant and friendly, I was taken advantage of. If I tried to be business-like, people would think I was angry. (See the reference a few paragraphs back to the double standard for men and women in this area!)

On one occasion, when I was about seven months pregnant with my son (and visibly so!), we had military orders to move. In the middle of moving our things, the movers (both male) asked me if I would run to the store and get them some food.

Early on in my experience with the military, I'd been told, "Always watch the movers." Now they were asking me to leave them alone with my stuff, take my three-year-old child and my pregnant self and go run an errand for them! I did not go get them food, and that may be why they didn't give 100% on the job-leaving behind several of our boxes.

If my husband had been there, I believe their attitudes would've been different! While they may have been trying to take advantage of me because I was nice, the fact is some men don't respect or take women seriously just by virtue of them being women, which I find infuriating, and gross.

My question was: What was it about me that made them think that my running an errand for them would have been a possibility?

After some pondering, I realized a few things I had a habit of doing in general: 1) My words and behavior *showed* people I needed their acceptance, so they knew they had the upper hand. They knew they could speak to me and treat me as they wished because I needed their validation. Because I desired people's approval, if I asked someone to treat me differently or if I held them accountable for their behavior, I wasn't taken seriously. While I was *disempowered* by my need for people's acceptance, they were *empowered* by it!

I demonstrated my need to be liked by laughing at people's (possibly funny) jokes too easily, making sure everyone was happy, and being overly concerned with what they thought about me.

2) Because I was constantly externally focused, I was unaware of my true feelings and needs. Since I didn't know what I needed, how could anyone else possibly know and therefore do anything about it? When I expressed myself, my words were filled with doubt and lack of self-assurance. (No one is going to get onboard a ship with a captain who doesn't believe in themselves and is uncertain where they're going!) Of course, I wasn't taken seriously or respected!

3) When I did know what was in my heart, what my inner voice (God!), was telling me, I was too afraid to follow through if I thought it would mean losing the approval of others! I wasn't taken seriously

because *I didn't take my own needs seriously*! I didn't prioritize what God was leading me to do over my seeking validation from people. Sometimes when we wonder why people treat us the way they do, we need to realize it's because we've *allowed* it! I didn't take a stand or advocate for my own needs when doing so meant I might lose people's acceptance. I wasn't respecting and honoring what was important to me. How could I possibly expect respect from others!

The first step in getting respect and being heard is realizing that *people respond to us based on our energy*. In other words, what we believe about ourselves and how we view other people plays out in our words and body language.

If I don't believe I'm worthy and valuable unless I have your approval, my verbal and nonverbal signals will communicate that to you.

The second step in getting people to take you seriously is to *stop seeking external control and validation.* Stop basing your self-worth on the words, moods, or behaviors of others.

When my husband and I got married, I was the epitome of caring too much what other people thought of me. I would never have dreamed of confronting someone for their inappropriate behavior because I wanted to be liked and accepted by everyone!

When I stopped caring so much about what others thought and I stopped needing external approval and validation from every person

I met, I took another major step toward inner peace and freedom by learning assertive communication. I started to let people know how their words and actions were affecting me. Before, I was so timid and afraid that someone wouldn't like me that I didn't speak up when people were rude or treated me poorly. I was mad about it, though, and would go home and tell my husband what had happened!

My husband would ask, "Did you say something to the person?" My answer was always, "No," until finally, I got tired of ignoring my feelings and I began to communicate to people when I preferred to be treated differently. For example, if a cashier slammed my change on the counter instead of handing it to me, I started to speak up. At times, the person I confronted would say, "Oh, I didn't realize I'd done that. I apologize." Other times, the exchange ended in silence and stern looks!

(Since then, I've noticed that when I have a proactively positive approach with others, and a grateful attitude, there are far fewer occasions I need to assert myself. I don't have as many run-ins with negative people, and if I do encounter them, I'm not as deeply affected. A calm, pleasant tone of voice can soften some of the most rude, abrasive communicators I've come across. But I needed to go through a phase of firmly asserting myself to overcome my fear of people's judgment and my need to be liked and accepted by everyone. It was a necessary part of my process, and now I have the tools to quickly enforce boundaries if someone refuses to participate in mutually respectful interactions!)

Assertive communication was the beginning of my taking back my power by speaking my true feelings, not seeking external validation, and not fearing people. I started to see what the world would look like if I didn't care about getting the approval and acceptance of every person I met.

You know what? I began to feel good. I began to feel that I had the power to change my self-perception, *and* how I was treated, and it came from *inside* of me. I began to feel a healthy sense of self-respect. God is not a respecter of persons (see Romans 2:11). We're all on the same level. No person should ever make another feel that they're not as good as they are or aren't worthy of being treated with dignity.

I know of a nurse being pushed by a doctor for no reason other than that the doctor was angry, and the nurse was in his path. Ridiculous. And illegal. Many times, we don't speak up because there's a hierarchy of power, and we fear retaliation, such as being fired, for calling out an injustice. Part of the problem in healthcare is that we've been conditioned to think that doctors are *more valuable people* than others, but we're all the same in the eyes of Our Creator.

Know your value and if you need help asserting yourself, get help. Talk to your human resources department. File a police report. Find a friend or an organization that will support you.

Unfortunately, some people won't change their behavior until another person addresses it. In other words, they'll get away with as much as they can until someone sets a boundary.

I experienced this one night when I was working at a hospital as a nurse on a medical-surgical floor. As is protocol, when you're assigned patients for your shift, you go into their rooms and do a physical assessment. This entails asking them several questions, listening to their heart and lungs, checking their neurological function, looking at their skin, eyes, mouths and so on.

When I entered one patient's room, I introduced myself, made small talk and explained to him what I was there to do. His attitude was disgruntled from the moment I walked in. He sighed with displeasure. He looked at me glaringly. His responses to my questions were blunt. He asked me why every nurse he's had asks him the same questions and does the same things over and over. I relayed to him that this is standard procedure to monitor for any changes in his condition. I noticed his mood, but I ignored it. I tried to be as friendly as I could.

It seemed like the friendlier I got, the more unpleasant he became! Finally, tired of his attitude, I said, "You know what, Sir? You have the right to refuse anything we offer you. Do you want this assessment done or not?"

It was the strangest thing. After I confronted him for his attitude, his demeanor completely changed. He said calmly, "Well, if you have to do it, go ahead." I said, "Ok, then. Let's continue." I looked at my computer screen to select the appropriate boxes on his chart and he said, "I'm proud of you." I thought, "Oh boy, this keeps getting weirder!" I said, "What do you mean?"

He went on to tell me that I was the first nurse who called him out for his bad attitude. He said he'd come into the hospital through the emergency room, had gone on to the ICU (intensive care unit), the PCU (progressive care unit), and was now on this floor. He said, "No one else said a word to me about how I was treating them." I said, "If you knew you were treating people badly, why did you do it?" He said, "*Because no one stopped me.*"

In my mind, my jaw dropped! I thought, "Alright. Lesson learned!"

None of us is internally motivated to do the right thing all the time. Sometimes we need an outside force to act upon us for change to occur.

At times, we may do what's right simply because it's right, but other times, we do what we can get away with (i.e., exceeding the speed limit in the absence of law enforcement, hiding that purchase from our spouse, or in this man's case being rude and disgruntled)! However, as we grow in our relationship with Jesus, more and more we're led by The Holy Spirit to do the right thing even when no one is watching.

When we believe we're worthy of mutual respect and we don't need to be validated or accepted by every human on the planet, we have a firm foundation from which we're empowered to be assertive and set boundaries when necessary.

When we fear what others think of us, we don't have respect for ourselves, and others don't respect us. We set ourselves up to be easy targets. In other words, people who are controllers are drawn to those who want external approval because they're easily controlled. Not wanting to lose approval, those seeking external validation become people pleasers. People pleasers do what others want, say what others want, and go where others want-all at the expense of not being true to what's in our hearts-or never discovering what's in our hearts. (The truth is we've never been in an environment in which we've felt safe to share our true feelings and needs.)

People who are controlling and those who are controlled both have the same goal: a feeling of self-worth and value based on external factors-the approval of others and the control of others. If we aren't afraid of what people think of us, we can't be controlled by them. We're set free from being people pleasers.

When I confronted people or requested that their attitudes or actions be different, I had no control over their response to my request. What they chose to do wasn't up to me. The important part for me was that I was beginning to face my fear of not being validated or liked by others. Speaking up was a good start!

When we stop caring about getting approval and acceptance from everyone, and we set boundaries, we become a powerful voice that helps others have the confidence to discover their value and ask for mutual respect. It's a beautiful thing to see our courage to own our self-worth ignite that same courage in someone else.

Our boundaries take care of themselves when we don't look for validation from other people. When we don't need approval from others, we're not vulnerable to being controlled and manipulated.

Our boundaries take care of themselves when we realize we have just as much right to be on Earth as every other person. We learn that we teach people how to treat us. We learn to ask for mutual respect. No one deserves to be treated as "less than" for any reason.

Mindsets to Move Forward

People raised in an atmosphere of anger, fear, control, and manipulation don't learn to have healthy boundaries. Even after the freedom I found in being assertive, sometimes my peace is threatened with thoughts about how someone might judge me or disapprove of me.

Abuse weakens our resolve because we start to believe we need approved and validation from others, but in 2 Corinthians 12:10, Jesus told Paul, "My grace is sufficient for you, for my power is made perfect in weakness." We are weak, but Our God is strong! Keep seeking Him!

It's a daily task to renew our minds to who we are in Christ Jesus-to remind ourselves that our worth and value doesn't come from others, but from God, The Creator of The Universe. How beautiful is that! My peace comes from my Creator's love for me. Let that soak into your heart. How beneficial it is to wake up each morning with this on our minds!

If I change my behavior based on what I think others are thinking about me, I'm seeking external validation, and am, in essence, voluntarily giving away my inner peace.

We're easily controlled and manipulated when we seek external approval, looking outside ourselves for peace and validation. Other people sense our need for their approval and don't take us seriously.

It takes a lot of discipline and inner strength to hold still when I feel the pull to *do* something or *say* something to get people to like me or approve of me. But change happens when we learn to maintain stillness instead of acting out of fear of not being accepted or approved of.

When we're not feeling well physically, for example, or if we feel overly responsible for other people, we're more vulnerable to having flimsy boundaries, but by maintaining the mindset, "I'm responsible for me and everyone else is responsible for themselves," I have a firm foundation on which to base my actions.

The Power of "No"

Practice boundaries by being prepared that when you ask someone a question, the answer may be "No." For example, if we want to give someone a hug, it's important to ask permission and never assume the answer will be "Yes"!

Physical affection is one of my love languages, but it isn't everyone's, and especially if someone has been physically traumatized, the last thing I want to do is make them feel like they don't have a choice. In asking permission, we model to others-and remind ourselves-that it's *vital* to set and respect boundaries. Saying "No" is a way to get our power back, especially after we've given it away-or had it taken-for too long!

The King James Version (KJV) of 2 Timothy 1:7 says, "For God has not given us a spirit of fear, but of power and of love and of a sound mind."

Be brave and say "No" to people who try to control or manipulate you into doing something that's not in your heart. This could be as simple as saying "No" to someone who asks you to be their partner on a project. You might have your own idea for the assignment. Saying "No" is a practice in being true to what's in your heart and to stop caring what others think of you.

Do something kind just for yourself, not because of how many "likes" the picture will get on social media, not because of what others will think, but simply because *you* like it; it makes *you* happy. Listen to a song you enjoy. Eat your favorite food. Call a friend. Take a walk. Paint a picture. Paint your toenails. Whatever it is, do it *only* for yourself-no thoughts of what others will think, no pressure to perform. You can begin to *give yourself* the love and respect that you've been looking for from others.

Practice assertive communication with a friend. Role play some scenarios you've experienced or are anticipating. Practice eye contact and confident body language. Research some methods you want to try.

It can be very difficult to follow our instincts when doing so may be seen as rude or otherwise outside social expectations, but freedom from needing approval from others can give us the courage to be socially *unacceptable* when necessary to protect ourselves-or our families!

God's Voice

For too long, I ignored my inner voice, God's voice, to get approval from people. I allowed my inner promptings, what was important to me, to be brushed past and treated as insignificant. I didn't advocate, or take a stand for, what God was speaking to me.

I wasn't taken seriously because I didn't respect or take myself seriously. I cared more to be accepted by people than I did to follow God's voice.

Mutually beneficial relationships allow each person to be true to what God has put in them without fear of losing the other person's approval. If you have relationships in which people do not support your following what God has put in your heart, if they try to manipulate you to do what they want or go where they want by acting sad, defeated, downcast, or angry when you tell them, "No, God has put something else in my heart," those aren't people you need in your corner! (If you want to keep them in your corner, firm boundaries need to be established!)

I've had relationships in which if I did my own thing, had my own course, and it wasn't to the other person's liking, they manipulated me to take their path–to do what they wanted. And because I wanted their approval, I altered my behavior and allowed myself to be controlled so that I wouldn't lose their acceptance or their friendship.

John 12:42-43 says, "But because of the Pharisees they would not confess their faith for fear they would be put out of the synagogue; *for they loved praise from men more than praise from God* [emphasis added]."

How do we ensure we follow our hearts and respect our boundaries concerning what God is speaking to us?

The answer is that we care more for the approval of God than the approval of man. God loves us and approves of us no matter what, but that doesn't mean He approves of everything we *do*. Once His Holy Spirit is in us, we have an urgency to follow His lead and we don't feel His peace if we don't follow what He has put in our hearts.

Following what God has put in your heart *is* seeking God's approval. Following what God has put in your heart is wanting God's approval more than man's approval.

Stop ignoring what's important to you to get validation from others. God made you. He puts desires in your heart based on His purposes for your life and He speaks to your spirit and prompts you accordingly.

I pray that we would not ignore what God has laid on our hearts to make someone else happy or to get, or keep, their approval. I pray we would have a fire in our spirits that burns with the desire to go where God leads us regardless of who approves.

Chapter 9

Moving Away from "Should"

It's important to our healing that we get clear about the difference between what we've been taught we *should* do and what's in our hearts.

When we lack an inner sense of identity (the peace, safety, and security that we get from the knowledge of God's unconditional love for us), we grasp at anything we can think of to earn acceptance and approval from others. With our hearts hardened and closed off from our true emotions, we make choices that we deem are socially acceptable-the choices that win us external approval-smiling when we aren't actually happy; saying "Yes" to an invitation because we don't want to be seen as antisocial; saying "Yes" to working extra hours because we think that will make our boss like us and possibly secure our position at work. (The reality is: Management does what's necessary to make businesses run. Working extra hours won't stop the company from terminating your position if it's in their best interest to do so!)

The most important factor in your healing is to be honest about your feelings. If you're sad, don't rush past the reason. Talk it out. Journal it out. If your heart is heavy, ask yourself why. Get to the root of the emotions that keep coming up.

Religious "Shoulds"

Religion tells us many things we *should* or *should not* be and *should* or *should not* do if we're Christians. For years I was externally motivated to do all the things Christians *should* do. I did what I thought would get me accepted and approved of by other Christians. I didn't want to draw attention to my struggles because I was taught that Christians are always joyful, polite, peaceful-never angry, irritated, hot-tempered. My experience had been that Christians will tell you what you should and shouldn't do and will judge you accordingly. So, I hid the best I could and stayed stuck in emotional hell.

We don't get free when we're judged, shamed, and condemned. We get free when we're shown love and nonjudgement. Jesus didn't come to condemn, or disapprove of, the world (John 3:17) and we shouldn't judge others. Romans 2:1 says, "…at whatever point you judge the other, you are condemning yourself…."

We need to be more aware of the reasons for people's mindsets and behaviors and accept them where they are.

A Christian with unhealed wounds (traumas) isn't necessarily going to be all the things religion says we *should* be.

The joy and happiness that some Christians experience right away after accepting Jesus into their hearts takes more time for others to realize. If this is your experience, it doesn't mean you're any less of a Christian. It doesn't mean you're not saved. When we believe in what Jesus came to Earth to do (redeem us from our sinful, human nature), we're sealed with the Holy Spirit (see Ephesians 1:13) and we are *working out* our salvation (see Philippians 2:12). 1 Corinthians 1:18 says we, "…are *being* [emphasis added] saved…."

Let go of what your healing *should or should not* look like according to religious edicts set by humans. Jesus healed on the Sabbath (see John 9:14) against what religious leaders of his day held as "right." In Isaiah 29:13, God expresses His displeasure with people whose, "'…worship of me is made up only of *rules taught by men* [emphasis added].'"

Religion is rules taught by men, but God is bigger than religion. He is Spirit, and His Spirit will do His will.

Authentic Giving

Just as you cannot export what you do not possess, you cannot pour from an empty cup. What does that mean? You can't give to others what you don't have yourself! If you want to be an authentic giver of God's love, you have to experience God's love for yourself. 1 John 4:19 says, "We love because he *first* [emphasis added] loved us." To show God's love to others, we need to cultivate a relationship with Him. Then, filled with His love, we have a *desire* to love others.

Many of us are taught, whether through religion or not, to give of ourselves to others-to live in service to others, but there's a difference between giving only because we think we "should," and giving because we've been so filled with God's love that our cups run over. Authentic giving takes place when we have an internal motivation, fueled by God's love in our hearts, to share His love with others. Giving to get approval and acceptance or to feel good about ourselves is a form of control and manipulation.

For example, when we give someone a compliment to try to get them to like us, we're trying to control their perception of us. When we give a compliment from the heart, it feels different. We don't have an expectation of getting anything in return. When giving is authentic, the person we give to doesn't feel a weird, controlling energy-as if we expect something back. They don't feel that we're empty and searching for validation of our worth; they feel that we're giving out of an overflow.

In Exodus 35:5, God told Moses to ask, "...everyone who is *willing* [emphasis added] ...," to gather the supplies needed to build the Tent of Meeting. Several times in chapters 35 and 36, we read *freewill* offering. In Exodus 35:21, we read, "...everyone who was *willing* and *whose heart moved him* [emphasis added] came and brought an offering to the Lord...." God wants us to give what's in our hearts to give. He wants *authentic* offerings-not what we feel we "should" do because everyone else is doing it.

There's healing power in being honest with what's in our hearts, even if it seems socially unacceptable. If we lie to ourselves and do what we think we *should*-when it's not in our hearts to do it-how will we ever uncover our truth? What is our truth? Our truth is the *why* in *why* we think the way we do and *why* we feel the way we do. But if we lie to ourselves out of fear of judgement, we deny ourselves the opportunity to discover the mindsets that got us here. If we don't know the *reasons* for what we think and feel, how can we heal? (By *reason*s, I don't mean necessarily that we have to relive every traumatic thing that's ever happened to us. But to get free, we need to look at the *messages* we received and have believed about ourselves as a result of the words and actions of others.)

When we do what we think we *should*, but it's not in our hearts to do it, our motivation is to get acceptance and approval from others, or to try to *earn* love. But when we have the courage to listen to our hearts and be true to our internal motivations, we set ourselves free from needing external validation. When we're free from the need for external approval, we're free to hear clearly, and to *do* what the Holy Spirit leads us to do regardless of the opinions of others.

No one may have ever done before what you feel in your heart is right to do. There may not be a blueprint for it. People may give you advice about what they think you should do based on their experiences but have the courage to listen to the voice of God in *you*.

In Galatians, Paul talks about his calling from God. Chapter 1:15-17 says, "But when God, who set me apart from birth and called me by his grace, was pleased to reveal his Son in me so that I might preach him among the Gentiles, *I did not consult any man* [emphasis added], nor did I go up to Jerusalem to see those who were apostles before I was…." Paul trusted God's Holy Spirit in him!

At times, there's value in consulting with pastors and Christian brothers and sisters but have faith and step out when it's time for you to do what you *know* God told you to do. Not everyone will agree with you. Not everyone will understand what you're doing. But stay close to God. Keep reading your Bible and praying and He will bring you confirmation and peace when you're on the path *He* has for you.

~Know Your Strengths~

The Time I Was Low-Key Fired from The Hospitality Team at Church (And I Needed to Be!)

A few years ago, a lady at my church wanted me to get more involved. Without my awareness that I was being volunteered, I found myself on the hospitality team.

This task entailed providing food for the pastor, the worship team, and others who were also serving at church that day. There was a budget and a gentle urging to prepare homemade meals; although, premade dishes were also acceptable, but possibly less budget friendly.

For someone who's been raised thinking they have to perform for acceptance, there was a part of me that rebelled against the notion that I'd be judged on the quality of the food I brought, so there was no way I'd be making anything homemade and risk rejection!

My heart wasn't in this assignment. Sometimes I forgot I was supposed to bring food and ran to the store at the last minute trying to find things people might like while staying within the budget. My contributions were pitiful! I would've fired me too!

It wasn't that I was intentionally malicious, and I wasn't trying to be let go, but I didn't have the foresight or imagination to be a good fit for the hospitality team!

A few months after I was never again asked to bring food on Sunday morning (!), I took a spiritual gifts assessment. Here's a surprise: my lowest score was in (you guessed it!)-hospitality!

My highest score was in faith, which I didn't realize was a spiritual gift. It's listed as a *fruit of the Spirit* in Galatians 5:22, but I'd never thought of it as a spiritual gift. (Sometimes what's a strength for us, we don't recognize as a strength because we're with ourselves all the time and grow accustomed!) Learning that faith is a gift, I felt peaceful and comforted. The news resonated with me. It felt right that my service to God would be based on what He's given me! (This isn't to say that we're limited to just one spiritual gift or one area to serve, but honestly, I would've been happier and more fulfilled cleaning toilets than if I was on the hospitality team! And the recipients of the food would've been happier as well!)

The people who serve on the hospitality team now do a phenomenal job. They're in their element!

Know your strengths and weaknesses. If you don't like children, please don't volunteer to serve in the children's ministry!

Don't compare your talents/gifts with anyone else's. All of us have a place and a purpose. All of us are needed.

About a year ago, I was given the opportunity to serve on a team at church that fits my strengths and pools my life experiences. I'm happy and grateful for the opportunity, and it feels good to help!

Serving doesn't have to feel like drudgery! You're allowed to enjoy what you do! Move away from "should"!

Overcoming Shame

Religious *shoulds and should nots* come with a lot of shame. I've lived with so much shame in my life that there've been moments when I've felt ashamed *for not feeling shame*! In other words, I've had thoughts that tell me I should be ashamed for feeling positive and for thinking encouraging, life-giving thoughts about myself! How ridiculous is the devil!

Overcoming shame starts with not feeling bad or guilty for where you are in life or for enjoying life! You're allowed to feel good about yourself! You're allowed to claim your God-given place as a forgiven, loved, child of the King of kings and Lord and lords! You're allowed to hold your head up and put your shoulders back and not succumb to the lies the devil tries to get you to believe. THERE IS NO SHAME ON YOU!!

One of the quickest ways to shut down the shame the devil tries to convince you of is to praise the Lord. Say, "Thank You, Jesus, for dying on the cross to free me from my human nature. I know that because of You, I am not shamed, I am *approved*. Thank you for washing me clean with the blood of your sacrifice. Because of *You*, I am *holy and blameless* in God's sight! Thank you for your Holy Spirit.

Thank you for being close to the brokenhearted. Thank you for giving me a peace that passes understanding. I love You, God, and no weapon formed against me will prosper. You died so I could have abundant life, and I praise You and thank You for it. I accept the abundant life You gave me. God, You are so good. There is no one like You. You are the Ancient of Days, the King of kings, the Lord of lords, the Alpha and the Omega, the Beginning, and the End. Thank You that *I am Your child*."

God wants you to *enjoy* your life! If you decided to savor the delicious, warm comfort of your bed on a Saturday morning, don't feel bad that you slept in. Put a smile on your face and thank God you had the opportunity!

Some of us are tempted to feel guilty or ashamed if we don't always listen to Christian songs or Christian radio stations. If I don't like the feeling I get from a song on secular radio, I change the channel! There are many songs that don't happen to be Christian, but that capture joy, the celebration of life, and mindsets that can heal us.

Religion tells us, "Do this. Don't do that." But *relationship* is different than religion. When we have a relationship with Our Creator, we're led in our hearts by The Holy Spirit, and there's freedom to assess what pleases God and what doesn't. We can feel it.

When we begin to heal, we can tell the difference between the condemning feeling of shame and guilt that comes from thinking we're required to perform for God's love and acceptance, and the feeling of *conviction* by His Holy Spirit.

The more we seek Him, the more we learn to differentiate between the two. When God lives in your heart, let your heart lead you!

Sometimes people use shame to make us feel responsible for them-their moods, words, behavior. They know that if they can get us to feel responsible for them, they can control us.

Parents, don't shame your kids, making them feel accountable for yours or anyone else's emotions. This makes kids feel unsafe and insecure. It makes them feel they have to control something they were never meant to control-other people!

Don't guilt them then expect them to have a sincere desire to serve or give to others. They need to know they're absolutely not responsible for what other people choose to do. They're responsible for how they choose to behave. They need to know they're loved without conditions, and from a place of self-love, they'll *want* to give to and love others.

Obviously, we need to teach our children accountability for their actions and to apologize when they hurt people. There need to be consequences for intentional wrongs, and if purposely hurting others is a continuous behavior, it's vital to get to the root cause, seeking professional help when necessary.

But if we haven't intentionally harmed others, freedom lies in the place where we recognize that the actions, attitudes, and behaviors of other people are *their* responsibility.

When we realize that hurt people hurt people, we can free ourselves from thinking something is wrong with us or that we're the reason for other people's bad attitudes and ugly behavior. When we learn to have a detached view of others, we start to get free from feeling overly responsible for them. What do I mean by a "detached view of others"? This means that my sense of value and worth doesn't come from anyone else's words and actions. A detached view is realizing they're accountable for what they choose to say and do, and, if I haven't purposefully hurt them, their choices have nothing to do with me and everything to do with them.

We start to overcome shame when we learn to take responsibility for our feelings and for our healing and realize that everyone else is responsible for theirs! We begin to replace negative self-talk with positive. We start thinking of ourselves the way God thinks of us. He created me. I want His thoughts of me to be my thoughts of myself!

Romans 8:1 says, "Therefore, there is now no condemnation for those who are in Christ Jesus." You can let go of the shame, and the guilt, and the feeling that you have to *earn* love and approval. Jesus said in John 14:27, "Peace I leave with you; my peace I give you. I do not give as the world gives…."

What does this mean? First, we cannot earn God's love. He loved us while we were still sinners (see Romans 5:8). He didn't give us His love then threaten to take it back or withhold it from us if we don't perform perfectly. His love for us doesn't change based on our behavior. He doesn't give as the world gives.

If you ever received a gift from someone and they made you feel guilty for it, or that you owed them for it, or threatened to take it from you if you didn't live up to their standards, that's an example of how the world gives.

The world controls and manipulates by making us feel guilty, ashamed, and disapproved of. Because the devil steals, kills, and destroys, he wants us to feel guilty, ashamed, and condemned, but God loves, accepts, and forgives. In His awe-inspiring grace, He's given us the gift of His Son, Jesus Christ. We have simply to accept Him-exactly as we are because it's not about who we are or what we've done; it's about Who *He* is. Grace is the unmerited favor of God. We don't deserve it. We can't earn it. But He's given it!

When we accept Him, our identity is in Him and what He did for us out of His love for us. Because of Jesus, we are holy, blameless, and approved of! In 2 Corinthians 5:17, Paul tells us, "Therefore, if anyone is in Christ, he is a new creation; the old has gone, then new has come!" If you don't feel like a new creation, I understand that. Keep seeking God. Stop looking for acceptance and approval from people! Keep renewing your mind to the truth of His Word. As you do, He will reveal Himself to you and do works in you that no human can!

Mindsets to Move Forward

Some people say feelings aren't important. To that I say what my grandpa would've said, "Hogwash!" Or,"Bologna!" Two terms that mean, "Not true!" Why not?

God is Spirit. We can't see Him or touch Him, but we can *feel* Him.

Romans 10:9 says, "…believe in your *heart* [emphasis added] …." Verse 10 goes on to say, "For it is with your *heart* [emphasis added] that you believe and are justified…." It doesn't say believe with your mind! We don't fall in love with our minds! It's a feeling.

Feelings are the breadcrumbs that lead us to the thoughts and beliefs we've developed that keep us where we are or help us grow.

Set yourself free from religious ideas of what a Christian *should* feel. Only when we're honest with ourselves about our thoughts and feelings can we get to the roots of our beliefs and begin to replace lies with truth from God's Word.

The devil uses shame to keep us stuck and keep our focus off God. John 8:44 says, "…he [the devil] is a liar and the father of lies." Fight the devil's lies with truth of God's Word!

*We are holy, righteous, and redeemed (see 1 Corinthians 1:30).

*Hebrews 10:10, "…we have been made holy through the sacrifice of the body of Jesus Christ once for all."

*Romans 8:1, "Therefore, there is now no condemnation for those who are in Christ Jesus."

*I am the righteousness of God in Christ Jesus (see 2 Corinthians 5:21).

Know your motives in giving.

Don't give to try to feel worthy! You're already unconditionally loved and approved of by God! You can't get any more worthy than that!

Have the courage to be honest about what's in your heart.

Giving from a place of fullness instead of a place of lack keeps us from giving to get something in return. From a place of fullness, we're giving out of love. From a place of lack, we're giving to try to *earn* love, acceptance, and validation, or to get someone to do something for us in return.

Giving from a place of lack is giving away our power because we're giving to get something we may not get! In other words, we have no control over whether others will be able to deliver what we perceive we need from them. When we give to get something, we don't feel good about ourselves. There's an emptiness inside we're trying to fill, and we give to try to feel worthy and valuable-not knowing that we're already worthy and valuable because we were created by God and He loves us!

If you've read this whole chapter and thought, "What about Proverbs 11:25 that says, '…he who refreshes others will himself be refreshed'"?

I've experienced that refreshment when I've prayed for someone even though I was exhausted. After encouraging them, I wasn't tired anymore! We may not always *feel* like giving, but somewhere deep inside we know it's right.

But for those of us who've been indoctrinated with religious *shoulds* and *should nots*, we need time, wisdom, and discernment to heal from the shaming and condemning voices that tell us we're wrong if we don't give.

The point is, be aware of your intentions and know that you don't have to give to get acceptance, approval, or validation. You already have all those things from Your Creator!

Chapter 10

Human Limitations and The Holy Spirit

"You are all sons of God through faith in Christ Jesus, for all of you who were baptized into Christ have clothed yourselves with Christ. There is neither Jew nor Greek, slave nor free, *male nor female* [emphasis added], for you are all one in Christ Jesus."

~Galatians 3:26-28

None of us thinks or acts the way God does (see Isaiah 55:8). Our human thinking can put limitations on The Holy Spirit based on our views of what is socially appropriate. But God will go against social conventions to accomplish His purposes, so keep an open mind, a humble attitude, and a courageous spirit when you sense Him urging your heart!

In 1 Samuel 25, we meet a brave woman, Abigail, who did just that. Her husband Nabal was wicked and a fool. Verse 17 says, "[Nabal] is such a wicked man that no one can talk to him." Nabal refused to give food to the future King David and his men who'd provided protection for Nabal's shepherds.

Abigail knew this was wrong, and she had the means to act, so *she* prepared food and her servants and went to meet with David. Verse 19 says, "…she did not tell her husband…."

You might be thinking, "Wait. What? Ephesians 5:22 tells wives to submit to their husbands. What was she doing?!"

The religion in us might gasp in shock, shake our heads, and purse our lips together at the horror of such a thing, but religion is different than *relationship*. Religion says, "Do this; don't do that." In *relationship* with God, we're led by The Holy Spirit. In relationship with God we know that our connection with Our Creator comes first. We're not meant to submit to authority that goes against our Christian ethics.

Abigail understood this principle which is also demonstrated in the Book of Daniel Chapter 3 when Shadrach, Meshach, and Abednego refused to follow the king's command to worship other gods. You might think, "The king is in charge. He has authority. How could they refuse to follow the king's commands?," but Shadrach, Meshach, and Abednego knew what the king had ordered was wrong. It was against their relationship with God, and they knew they were to yield to *God's* authority before yielding to a *person's* authority.

It feels amazing to support and encourage our spouse when they're being led by God, but when they make wicked or foolish decisions, we cannot support or encourage their choices. To do so would be against our relationship with God.

Personally, I've suppressed an urge to act according to what I know is right because I believed I was meant to *always* submit to my husband. I was operating with a religious mindset that said, "Do this; don't do that," instead of being led by God's Holy Spirit. But God doesn't move within the confines of our limited, religious, human thinking, or our earthbound views of acceptable gender roles. He does what is necessary to achieve His plans.

There's a story in the Book of Judges illustrating that sometimes husbands are meant to follow the lead of their wives. In Judges 13:2-23, we meet Manoah whose wife is sterile and has no children. (Interestingly, her name is never given.)

An angel of the Lord appeared to her and told her she would have a son. The angel went on to give her instructions regarding the child.

When she went to her husband to tell him what had happened; he listened to her; he believed her; and he prayerfully supported the message she'd received from God!

Manoah prayed, asking God to teach them how to bring up the boy. This husband was humble, supportive, and had a heart to please the Lord.

What happens next is intriguing. After *Manoah* prayed, God heard his prayer and sent His angel again-to his *wife*! We read that Manoah was not with her when the angel arrived (verse 9). So, again, she went to her husband and told him what happened. Judges 13:11 says, "Manoah got up and *followed his wife* [emphasis added]."

Later, the woman advises her husband regarding spiritual matters. Manoah thinks they're going to die because they've seen an angel of God. He expresses this fear to his wife. (Note that he wasn't afraid to share with her the concern in his heart.)

In Judges 13:22, we see her advisement, "But his wife answered, 'If the Lord had meant to kill us, he would not have accepted a burnt offering and grain offering from our hands, nor shown us all these things or now told us this.'"

What a powerhouse couple! Both had a desire to please God and neither let cultural gender roles nor social conventions prevent them from hearing God, seeking Him, and following through on His plan for their lives.

These two became the parents of Samson, who, by pursuing God's promptings in *his* heart, helped fulfill the Lord's plan for His people at that time (see Judges 14:4).

My purpose in sharing this with you is that we would be led by God's *Spirit* and His purposes more than we are by limited human thinking that dictates our social norms and religious ideals.

Conforming to our human standards can cause us confusion and unnecessary angst when we feel The Holy Spirit moving us outside of those boundaries.

Limited human thinking entails the belief that if you're a man, you are by default a leader, serious, business like, non-emotional, physically, and mentally tough. Likewise, if you're a woman, human constructs have placed parameters on who and what you are simply by virtue of your gender. Restricted social thinking tells us that women are supposed to be followers, not to be taken seriously, submissive, timid, emotional, not physically strong.

Some men think women have nothing of value to offer in conversation-simply by virtue of their being female-and therefore, they will not heed their input.

What's my point? These are biases based on stereotypes. We need to outgrow the thinking that all men are "this" and all women are "that." We need to assess strengths and weaknesses on an individual basis and not on the grounds of gender. Gender bias limits our potential to heal, learn from each other, and grow in our relationship with God.

How? When a man thinks it's not a woman's "place" to give him spiritual advisement, he may miss overcoming an obstacle in his heart. Just as Manoah's wife spoke life-giving words of wisdom to him when he was worried, men, be aware that God may give your wife a message for you. Don't immediately dismiss a woman who has a word from God to speak into your life solely because she's a woman!

Mindsets to Move Forward

I have a passion (in cases you couldn't tell!) and a heart for the suffering of both men and women regarding expected social/gender roles. I'm addressing men here, but the spiritual principles apply to anyone who has wrestled with similar issues. You may think, "How can a woman know the struggles of a man?" The answer is because there is no male or female in Christ Jesus (see Galatians 3:28) and, as we learned above, when God has a message for His people, He gives it to whom *He* wants!

Men, don't put too much pressure on yourselves and believe you have to shoulder all your pain, grief, and concerns on your own. Do not conform to social gender roles regarding what is *manly* at the expense of your mental and physical health. There's no shame in admitting you're not mentally tough and emotionally strong all the time. Strength is telling the truth about the condition of our hearts-regardless of what that looks like to society or how you may be judged.

There's a social expectation that men aren't supposed to cry, and physical strength is rewarded. Some men think emotional vulnerability is weakness and punishable with shame and rejection. This both infuriates me and breaks my heart.

Men who adhere to these mindsets keep themselves and their fellow males in bondage to fear of man. They desire social approval more than pleasing God by letting Him into their hearts. (Women do this too! I was one of them.)

One of the fallacies that perpetuates this constrictive thinking is the belief that to protect our children from evil in the world, we have to "toughen them up," treat them harshly and without empathy, patience, compassion. But this leads only to hard-hearted children who live in a state of chronic stress and anger, propagate violence, and whose hearts are closed off to protect them from further abuse.

Being patient, calm, compassionate, and empathetic with kids builds strength in them. Kids do not become strong or potentially able to face any obstacle in life when we're abrasive, overly strict, tough (what some would say is "manly"). Resilience and a sense of security is what makes people strong and that's built with patience, gentleness, kindness-all the things love is. It doesn't make sense to our human minds that gentleness and kindness-things so precious, delicate, and peaceful to experience-would make us strong, but God's ways are not our ways, and His thoughts are not our thoughts (see Isaiah 55:8).

Jesus was fully God and fully man. In God, He is *The Creator of the Universe* (see John Chapter 1), and He came to Earth gentle and humble in heart (see Matthew 11:29). It doesn't make sense to our human minds that He came to *save the world* with gentleness and humility!

Chronic stress from harsh punishments and unkind, disapproving words will not create tough, resilient people. Love does that.

Romans 2:4 tells us, "…God's *kindness* [emphasis added] leads you toward repentance…."

Just as the gentleness and humility of The Creator of the Universe confound our human thinking, God uses our weaknesses to show His glory. He gives us desires we cannot accomplish in our human strength alone. Likewise, His design is that our hearts don't heal only by our human efforts. If we were able to do all God asked us to do, including mend our hearts in our own power, why would we need Him?

It's not our physical strength or (exclusively) our human endeavors that heal us and accomplish His purposes in us. Our hearts begin to change in a lasting way when we're humble and realize we're weak without God. Without His *supernatural* provision that confounds our human thinking, we can do nothing of significance. We don't heal in our own power or accomplish His plans for our life in our power. God mends our hearts and prepares our path in ways no human ever could.

One of the biggest lies of the devil is that we have to be perfect, have all our issues worked out, and have all the answers for God to use us, but God uses imperfect people (i.e., the author of this book!) to show who *He* is. We are *nothing* without Him. We are weak, but *He* is strong.

1 Corinthians 1:26-31 says:

"Brothers, think of what you were when you were called. Not many of you were wise by human standards; not many were influential; not many were of noble birth. But God chose the foolish things of the world to shame the wise; God chose the weak things of the world to shame the strong. He chose the lowly things of this world and the despised things-and things that are not-to nullify the things that are, so that no one may boast before him. It is because of him that you are in Christ Jesus, who has become for us our wisdom from God-that is, our righteousness, holiness and redemption. Therefore, as it is written: 'Let him who boasts boast in the Lord.'"

Don't stay stuck in pain and anger because you desire to please people and get their approval (by conforming to socially expected gender roles) more than you desire to please Your Creator. Don't let fear of being made fun of or having your "man card" taken if you show weakness, stop you from crying out to God, baring your heart to Him. (And ladies, don't be afraid you're conforming to gender expectations when you show emotion and cry because God touched your heart.

Who cares what people think! I'm not going to miss out on my healing out of fear of being judged by people who are stuck in limited human thinking!)

Because I'd felt weak and powerless around others for so long, I used anger and the hardness of my heart to protect myself from appearing vulnerable. I'd learned that when I'm vulnerable, I get hurt. That's the human way, right? We're angry, hard-hearted, and abrasive to others to make sure we don't get hurt anymore. But God's way doesn't make sense to the human mind. We think if we show weakness, we cannot protect ourselves. The truth is, *until* we admit we are weak without Him, we will *stay* hurt! God uses the weak things to shame the strong!

How? *He shows up when we show our weakness*. When we lay down our pride, our striving to keep the walls up around our hearts, our fear of what others think, our desire to get approval from others, our fear of appearing vulnerable, our belief that we can fix everything that's broken on our own, God says, "I've got you, child. *You* are weak, but *I* am strong."

1 Peter 5:5 says, "…God opposes the proud but gives grace to the humble." What does that mean? When we give Him our hearts in humility, admitting our human way has not yielded any significant, life-changing results, He gives us His grace. In 2 Corinthians 12:9, we

see that the Lord told Paul, "…My grace is sufficient for you *for my power is made perfect in weakness* [emphasis added]."

Weep. Release the heavy burden in your heart. You were never meant to fight alone or heal alone. God will never leave you or forsake you. He's as close to you as the heart in your chest.

He will urge your heart in the direction He wants you to go. Isaiah 30:21 says, "Whether you turn to the right or to the left, your ears will hear a voice behind you saying, 'This is the way; walk in it.'" Some of you may hear the audible voice of God, but when He speaks to me, it's a sense in my spirit of what He wants me to do. When we seek God with a sincere desire to know Him and follow His ways, we can trust that the ideas He gives us and the pull we feel inside to go to this place or talk to that person are His Holy Spirit guiding us. Be sensitive to His voice-the desires He puts in your heart.

Place your hand over your heart and thank Him for being with you. May you have the courage to lay down your fear of what others think, your need for approval from humans, and may you feel the peace and love of God in your heart like never before. For His glory and your peace and healing in Christ Jesus.

Chapter 11

Tell the Truth

He who conceals his sins does not prosper, but whoever confesses and renounces them finds mercy.

~Proverbs 28:13

It's sacred when people share what's in their hearts even when it isn't necessarily socially acceptable. It's sacred because truth sets us free! How? In telling the truth, we accept ourselves as we are, and acceptance frees us from the emotional burdens of fear of judgement, disapproval, shame, and rejection. When we accept ourselves as we are, we can clearly see where we want to make changes in our lives.

People aren't motivated to change by being made to feel guilty, ashamed, and disapproved of. True, lasting change is prompted by compassion, mercy, grace, and kindness. After all, it's the *kindness* of God that draws us to Him (see Romans 2:4).

An environment teeming with judgment, control, and manipulation causes us to fear being truthful about what's happening inside our hearts. Fear of being judged, disapproved of, and shamed is a big reason many people don't go to church, and the reason that we stay stuck.

Only when we feel safe can we be honest about what we're going through in life. A church should be a sanctuary of mercy and compassion, a place where God's love is tangible. (Mercy, compassion, and love doesn't mean we aren't held *accountable* for our actions, but there's a difference between accountability and the control and manipulation of shame, judgment, and condemnation.)

For a lot of us who were raised in church, we hold ourselves to unrealistic ideals that keep us in bondage. Our spiritual growth has been hindered by the belief that Christians are required to be always happy, joyful, have a smile on our faces and NEVER be angry-as if we have to portray to the world that since we believe in Jesus, we don't have any problems or need any healing. This thinking comes from shame and religious judgment and plainly is not true. We're all *working out* our salvation (see Philippians 2:12) and every person on this planet has sinned and fallen short of God's glory (see Romans 3:23). That's the entire reason for Jesus!

Our belief in, and acceptance of Him, into our hearts doesn't immediately deliver us from the effects of the trauma we've lived and the hell we've walked through, but my belief in, and my relationship with, My Creator gives me *hope* for my healing because *He is our*

Healer. Psalm 147:3 says, "He heals the brokenhearted and binds up their wounds."

The more I get to know Him, the more He restores me. The more I speak His Word into my life, the more He mends my heart. Healing doesn't happen by hiding or ignoring what's in my heart. God uses our thoughts and feelings to bring our attention to areas in us He wants to repair. If we hide our true thoughts and emotions because we're ashamed of them (or fear we'll be judged for them), we prevent Him from reaching those painful places and we stay in pain. Healing happens when I'm honest about the state of my thoughts and feelings, and I cry out to God believing He will restore me.

To get free, it's essential that we're truthful with ourselves about the feelings that come up in us. Following the trail of our thoughts and feelings, assessing them, and asking ourselves what the reasons are we have them is crucial on our path to freedom. Ephesians 4:25 says, "Therefore each of you must put off falsehood and speak truthfully to his neighbor…"

Are you angry all the time? No judgment. It's okay. What is *not* okay is taking your anger out on others by yelling, hitting, being passive aggressive, or otherwise abusive to any living creature. All these behaviors deny our responsibility for our feelings and keep us from growing and changing. Ephesians 4:26 says, "In your anger, do not sin…." So, what do we do with our anger? We find healthy ways to cope with it as we learn more self-control.

Take a break from the situation. Learn to say, "I'm feeling really angry, and I don't want to hurt anyone with my words or actions, so I need some time to myself." You may need to scream, cry, hit a heavy sack, run, call a mentor, journal. Ask yourself what happened in that moment that caused you to have such an intense reaction. A seemingly disproportionate reaction to a current event is likely because it reminds you of a time when someone hurt you and you couldn't defend yourself.

If we were put in stressful, abusive situations as children, we were powerless to protect ourselves. All rational thought was shut down by fear and we were left confused and completely overwhelmed by an enormous weight of shame and anger that created an emotional, psychological, and physical blockage in us. (For more on these effects see Chapter 14.) We felt completely defenseless and literally out of control. There was nothing we could have said or done to protect ourselves.

Now, when faced with situations we find emotionally or physically threatening, we explode in rage. Anger is the only way we know to gain control of circumstances and people to ensure our safety. We need to make sure we aren't going to get hurt again.

We need to make sure people aren't judging us negatively, so if we *have* exploded in rage, we blame others, or the situation, for our reaction.

Reverting to our childhood need to be taken care of, we may purposely put ourselves in a position where we have to be rescued (i.e., intentionally taking a wrong turn while driving hoping someone in the car will pay attention to us and save us, correcting our mistake).

Lacking a sense of internal power and control, we may become passive aggressive to feel empowered (i.e., ignoring others when they speak, arguing about small, insignificant details, being condescending), or we may feel a need to have all the answers.

When we think that the amount of knowledge we have is a direct reflection of how worthy we are, we talk like we know everything and argue when others have a different opinion. Our mind is always working on how what someone else says is wrong and the way we see things is right. Arguing is a way we feel empowered when we don't have an internal sense of security, safety, and peace.

(I'm not saying never argue! An argument grounded in logic can yield creative and unconventional solutions! I'm saying to be aware of your intentions. Are you sincere about solving a problem? Or are you arguing because you don't feel valuable unless you're the one with the answers?)

Sometimes an over-the-top, excessive reaction is because we have a fear of abandonment. Our caregivers weren't there for us physically or emotionally when we needed them. Maybe your caregiver was physically present, but they didn't have the capacity to be available to you for your emotional or relationship needs.

My first realization that I had abandonment issues came shortly after my husband and I were married. He was still on active duty in the Army and was therefore required to be away for weeks at a time to conduct training. On one occasion when he was gone, I remember waking up during the night and sitting bolt upright in bed. Breathing heavily, I searched the dark room for him. When I remembered where he was, I was overcome by a sense of loneliness and a heavy feeling in my chest.

I remember thinking how strange it was that I was affected that way, but it's natural that our childhood wounds surface in our adult relationships. This experience made me realize that the underlying reasons for my emotions in my relationship with my husband had a basis in past occurrences in my life.

Ask God to show you the reasons for your emotions. We may be accustomed to using anger to control and intimidate others because we're afraid that if we don't have control of them, they'll leave us, but we aren't meant to control other people. If someone is staying with us only because they're afraid to leave, that isn't love. The Bible says in

1 John 4:18, “There is no fear in love. But perfect love drives out fear….”

Telling the truth is the beginning of taking responsibility. Taking responsibility for our emotions means we stop focusing our energy outward (on controlling others) and we start holding ourselves to a higher standard of behavior. We start becoming accountable for our words and actions, and that begins with knowing the *reasons* for our thoughts and feelings.

Why? Our thoughts and feelings drive our behavior. When we know the underlying causes of our actions, we’re empowered with self-awareness and logic. From a place of logic, we’re no longer driven by internal chaos, confusion, fear, and anger. From a place of logic, we understand our experiences have laid the groundwork for how we are, and restoration is not going to come from controlling and manipulating other people. Restoration comes when we *turn inward* and take responsibility for our role in our healing.

When I was in my anger addiction, I would yell at my children or husband for something (likely trivial), and while I felt relieved by the release of emotion, at the same time, I felt awful that I’d hurt my family.

Only when my heart was broken by how my actions were affecting them did I begin to make a different choice. In those moments that I used to blow up, I learned to shut my mouth-for no reason other than that I was committed to not hurting my family anymore. I slowly began to learn to *talk* about my feelings instead of *acting* them out.

Was it uncomfortable? Yes. I felt fire like a capsule of explosive energy in my chest almost constantly. I didn't always understand the reasons I was so angry. Some of it was probably habitual patterns of reacting I'd learned from an early age. Whatever the cause, *I* was responsible for my healing.

When your heart is buried in hurt and pain, it's blocked off from how your words and actions make other people feel. This is the reason that one of the first things I pray for people who are angry and whose words and actions are hurting others is that their hearts break with the things that break God's heart. My broken heart was the first step in the beginning of lasting change for me.

I pray our hearts are broken with tenderness and humility and we begin to feel compassion for ourselves and compassion for others. Hearts broken with tenderness and humility are different than hearts broken and *hardened.* Broken hearts can quickly become *hardened* hearts because of fear of judgment, shame, anger, guilt, and humiliation from the trauma and hell we've walked through. But to start to heal, we have to let go of the hard shell we've built to protect ourselves. Psalm 95:7-8 says, "…Today if you hear his voice, do not harden your hearts…."

Healing requires sincere remorse for our actions, and an honest assessment of our thoughts and feelings. To admit we want to change shows meekness and gentleness of heart. The Bible says in Matthew 5:5 that the meek will "inherit the earth." How? We humble our flesh (the earth) by recognizing we don't want to continue living in anger and pain, hurting ourselves and others with our words and actions, and we allow God in His *supernatural* power to work in us.

When we seek God and give Him our hearts-no matter how broken or hardened-in Him, we inherit victory over our human, fleshly, earth nature. Little by little He does works in us *by His Spirit* that no human could ever do!

The second step is to be bold and tell the truth about what you feel-no matter how ugly or socially unacceptable. Why? Because what we resist persists. What do I mean by that? If I don't admit I have a problem, nothing changes. If I don't look at myself and face my thoughts, feelings, and behaviors head on, I will continue to do what I've always done, and never learn what motivates my behavior.

The third step is taking responsibility for ALL our thoughts and feelings-regardless of the reasons we have them-and for our behaviors. Our accountability empowers us to take steps to change. We are *not* responsible for causing the pain and anger we feel inside, and the thoughts and feelings we have as a result, but we are 100% responsible for how we choose to behave.

Mindsets to Move Forward

1) List emotions you've had difficulty dealing with. What does each of these emotions feel like in your body? Is there a heaviness in your heart? A tightness in your lower back? Knowing where in our bodies we carry these emotions can help us become self-aware, which helps us own what we're feeling. Try taking a deep breath into these tight or heavy areas.
2) How do you respond to these emotions? Do you yell? Say hurtful things? Break things? Hit people? The Bible says in Ephesians 4:26, "In your anger, do not sin…." Anger is not wrong, but our responses to it can be.
3) Think about how you'd like to behave differently the next time this hard emotion comes up for you. Rehearse in your mind the response you'd like to have.
4) Pray that God breaks your heart with the things that break His heart. Find new ways to deal with tough emotions. What are your ideas for making this change? Exercise? Journaling? Find a mentor who manages their anger well and ask them what their strategy is.

*Be aware of the following and be courageous to admit if you struggle with these areas like I did. When we tell the truth, we set ourselves free!

*Angry people have been victimized, and we're scared we'll be hurt again. We seek restoration for the victimization. We use anger to make people feel afraid and responsible for our moods and behavior. We make them feel ashamed by blaming them for our thoughts and feelings. We feel safe only when we're in control of people and circumstances. When we don't take responsibility for ourselves, we're passive aggressive, taking power from others. We feel justified for our angry outburst when we can bait someone else into exploding in anger as well.

*When we're angry and don't take responsibility for our words and actions, we develop feelings of entitlement. We feel that the person we're angry with *owes us* **because** we're angry. In the past, someone else *did* owe us for the wrong done and we were never compensated for it. Our current anger and feelings of entitlement are a way we look for a resolution for the past injustice. But to claim our power to make our lives what we want them to be, we alone must take ownership of our feelings. For example, when we're angry, we can learn to make statements that keep *us* responsible for what we're thinking and feeling. We can say, "When you interrupt me, *I feel* that my point of view isn't important to you." Then ask for the change you want. Say, for instance, "I would feel loved, cared for, respected, if you wait until I'm finished talking." (Be open to others asking you for what they need as well!)

* We aren't always responsible for our wounds in life, but we are always responsible for our healing. This is one of the toughest truths we must face to grow and change and ultimately make our lives what we want them to be.

Your healing is more important than what people think about you.
God already knows all your thoughts and feelings.
Don't let shame stop you from crying out to Him.
There is NO SHAME on you in the eyes of Your Creator (see Romans 8:1)!
God loves you unconditionally-NO MATTER WHAT!
Your heart is safe in His hands.

Chapter 12

Responsibility

Responsibility is defined as the state or fact of having a duty to deal with something or of having control over someone; the state or fact of being accountable or to blame for something; a thing that one is required to do as part of a job, role, or legal obligation; the opportunity or ability to act independently and make decisions without authorization.[1]

One of the hardest, but most beautiful and liberating, aspects of recovering from emotional abuse is realizing that we alone have the power to change ourselves. Our health, mental well-being, every part of our lives, is now blissfully, (and at times overwhelmingly!) our responsibility. We are accountable for ourselves. We have the power to make our lives what we want them to be, meaning that our ability to feel inner peace, safety, and security is not dependent upon anyone but ourselves.

The nature of abuse is that we have no control over what happens to us. Other people said or did things to us that we didn't said or done, and we had no power (physical or verbal) to stop them. We learned that we're *not* responsible for ourselves; someone else determined our circumstances.

Having been treated this way, many of us have developed a pattern of thinking that doesn't serve us well in life. We begin to think that we don't have control of, or responsibility for, ourselves. Our circumstances have been such that time after time we had no choice. Someone else took our power from us-our power to say "Yes" or "No," our power to decide what we wanted to happen. Our self-esteem, self-worth, sense of safety, sense that we have the ability to make our lives what we want them to be, were taken from us. It's the most evil sort of robbery.

Of course we're angry! We never should have been hurt the way we were and now, here we are in the mire and muck of it all-emotionally, mentally, and (usually) physically-suffering for the wrongs that have been done to us. What happened to us is *not* our fault. The abuser(s) are 100% responsible for their actions. The issue, though, is that if we want to take back power over *our* lives, *we* have to do the work to be accountable for all our thoughts and feelings. No, we are not responsible for causing the pain and anger inside, but if we want to experience peace and joy in life, *we* have to take ownership of what's going on in our hearts and minds. *You* are the only one with the power to change *you*.

Unfortunately, as long as we blame another person (and yes, they are at fault!) for our feelings and state of being, we give away our power to change. As long as we think that our control lies outside of ourselves, we deny our God-given ability to make our lives what we want them to be. In other words, we don't have to live controlled by what happened to us in the past. Did the words and actions of others cause us to view ourselves as unworthy and unlovable? Yes. Did the abuse cause us to have skewed perceptions of what God intended to be holy and enjoyable? Yes. Can we heal from the evil that was done to us? Yes!

There is hope and it starts with the awareness that I am-as William Ernest Henley penned in his famous, originally untitled, poem, "…the master of my fate and the captain of my soul."[2] (This poem would later be named *Invictus*,[3] a Latin word meaning, *unconquered*.) What does this mean? This means that regardless of what we've suffered in life, as long as we're still breathing, we can turn the righteous and justified anger we feel into fuel that empowers us to make the changes we want.

One of the hardest things to do in life is take responsibility for our healing when we are *not responsible* for the damage that was done!

How do we do that? It starts in the present with becoming aware of our feelings and then being accountable for them instead of blaming them on anyone else-no matter what they've done.

If someone cuts me off in traffic, *I* am responsible for the feelings I have as a result of that. Incidentally, I'm also culpable for my actions that ensue because of those feelings. The other person did not "make me" curse, flip them off, or honk my horn. Those actions were all *choices* I made based on my feelings. No one "makes" us do anything. "Look what you made me do," is a familiar sentiment, but it's illogical, and a way people try to manipulate us into feeling guilty or responsible for something we are NOT responsible for-someone else's feelings, words, or actions.

Once we learn that we're responsible for ourselves, it's like we just opened a powerful gift. Our ability and potential to make our lives what we want them to be is up to us. Life becomes fun, enjoyable, full of hope and wonder-maybe for the first time ever.

One of the obstacles we face on our path to empowerment is known as l*earned helplessness*. This occurs when children, for example, tried to tell their caregivers that something evil was happening to them, but they didn't have the vocabulary to describe it, they weren't believed, or worst of all, the caregiver knew and did nothing to protect the child. (I'm using children as an example; however, strong, adult women and men have also become so worn down by devasting words and actions that they've felt powerless over their own lives. Abuse can be insidious-slowly poisoning the heart and rendering us defenseless. It's not right, and it should never happen to anyone.)

Learned helplessness causes us to think that no matter what we do, nothing is going to change. It causes us to think that we have no control over our lives or what happens to us. We become accustomed to other people deciding what's acceptable for us to think, feel, say, or do. We become disempowered and we lose ourselves, or we don't even get to know ourselves.

Constantly worried about the possibility of emotional or physical harm, we didn't get to experience the calm, quiet reflection that is afforded to people who live in peace and safety, not worried that every move they make is wrong or being scrutinized. Learned helplessness causes us to look outside ourselves for feelings of safety and security. If mom or dad is happy, we're safe. If they aren't, we need to have our guard up.

Once we're safe and no longer in an abusive environment, we can begin to heal. We can begin to get to the root of the messages that have been planted in our hearts. We have to know what we believe about ourselves and the world around us. Why? Knowing what we believe makes us aware of areas in our hearts that need our attention.

To begin to break down the walls around our hearts, we need to start looking at our feelings, no matter how embarrassing we think it is to feel the things we do. This work helps us piece together the reasons for our thoughts and actions. We start to see the motives in our hearts. We start to understand that we feel illogical rage when a certain thing happens because it reminds us of a time when we were powerless to change our circumstances.

Feelings are messages. It's vital to our healing and well-being that we notice them and investigate their source. What happened to us that triggers that emotion? What beliefs do we have about ourselves that cause us to feel shame, embarrassment, or that we're not worthy or valuable but everyone else somehow is?

What we believe dictates what we think and what we think becomes our actions. It's imperative to know what we think about ourselves. Our feelings are the clues that lead us to the source of our beliefs. Get curious. Ask questions of yourself. Why do I feel this? Is this a recurring thought/emotion for me? Does this feeling accompany anything in particular-a scene or a situation? Is there a pattern that keeps showing up?

Back in my angry days, I didn't like to see happy children. I can imagine some of you may gasp in shock after reading that. I know. It's weird that an adult would think something like this, but my goal is to tell the truth to help others get free!

The truth is, I was jealous of these seemingly happy kids because their parents were available to them and met their emotional needs. It hurts to see people get what we needed but weren't given. (Before you call for the pitchforks and stakes, know that today I feel joy flow in my heart and can't help but smile when I see happy children and parents who are being good to them!)

But I had to process my anger to heal from it. When you are in process, be humble and aware of your feelings. Don't judge yourself for anything that comes up for you. Be gentle with yourself and make note of your feelings, but don't attach to them and get down on yourself because, for example, as in my case, no one should be jealous of little kids! There's a reason you feel what you do. Explore it and learn from it. I'm very thankful for parents, who after suffering mistreatment in their own childhood, chose to discover a better way to raise their children.

To smooth your journey, take care of your physical self. Empower yourself with a daily routine that includes spending time with God, exercise, and healthy food. Guard your heart and mind in Christ Jesus by staying thankful, and as much as is possible, keep away from people who drain you!

We're all responsible for our health and well-being. It's exciting and fun to realize that, while at the same time, I understand it can be overwhelming and new territory. You may feel shaky, like a baby horse just learning to use its legs. Hang in there. Do the work and before you know it, you'll feel stronger and have more confidence and inner peace.

You may know you don't want to stay where you are, but the way forward is to accept yourself as you are right now. What we resist persists. Our pain must be validated. When we pretend we're fine, but we're not really fine, we're resisting what needs to be looked at for us to begin to heal.

Take some time to check in with yourself and see what's going on in your heart and mind. Journal. Assess your thoughts and feelings. If you feel nothing but numbness and heaviness where you know your heart is, say that. The key is to be honest with yourself exactly where you are. The truth sets you free-layer by layer-and eventually you will feel something besides anger or numbness and heaviness in your chest.

Be kind and nonjudgmental toward yourself. Whatever you're feeling is okay. You don't have to prove anything to anyone else. This is *your* healing. Tell yourself the truth. Be honest with *you*. Keep your journal in a safe place so that it's for your eyes only.

Seek professional help when you need it. Talk to a pastor. Talk to a counselor. Join a support group for codependency or anger. The National Mental Health Hotline is 988. It isn't a weakness to ask for help. We're self-aware and very brave when we look inside ourselves, want to change, and know that we need help to do so. Wherever you are on your healing journey is okay. Some days it may feel like you've made two steps forward and other days it feels like you have gone backward five steps. It's okay. Be gentle with yourself. All of it is progress. Don't compare your journey to anyone else's. Don't let anyone tell you where you *should* be by now. That isn't up to them; it's up to you.

If others pass judgment, telling you where you *should* be, say, "That's one way to look at it." If they won't let it go, keep repeating, "That's one way to look at it." What does this do? This keeps us from getting emotional about someone else's opinion. Don't let the opinion of another have a negative hold on you and keep you from progressing. You don't have to prove yourself to anyone else. You don't have to be where they say you *should* be. This is YOUR healing and 100% your responsibility. You're doing the work, not anyone else.

This isn't to say that we don't have to earn back trust in relationships. When we've said and done hurtful things to our loved ones, when our moods, attitudes, and behaviors have kept them in fear, we need to let them know that we're working to change. We need to apologize when we get angry and act it out instead of talking it out. This is a journey. They will see you changing little by little, and little by little, their trust will begin to grow as their hearts heal.

None of us set out to cause pain to our loved ones. But hurt people hurt others. We need to heal ourselves so we can become people who love themselves and can love others.

When our families and friends know that we're hurting, they sometimes want to press "fast forward" and see us healed and happy right away! But healing is a process. Be patient with yourself. Keep doing the work. Sometimes the work is to be silent and just *be*. Keep trusting God. God makes everything beautiful in HIS time (Ecclesiastes 3:11).

Mindsets to Move Forward

In the past, if you've felt powerless to ask for what you need in relationships, you can begin today to own your power to make changes by taking responsibility for *yourself*-your thoughts and feelings. What is the belief behind them? Once you know that, you can trace back the way you were treated and the words that were spoken about you to understand where the beliefs came from. Aware of the cause, you can begin to replace lies with truth.

The truth is you are worthy, unconditionally loved, and a child of The Creator of the Universe. You have just as much worth and value as everyone else on Earth. You are worthy of mutual respect. Believing the truth, your thoughts and feelings will begin to line up and you'll be empowered to ask for what you need in your relationships. There is no need to throw a fit, bait people, or blame others for how you're feeling to get your needs met.

One practical way to communicate our needs is to say, "I've noticed (a particular behavior that makes you feel disrespected, for example), and I'd appreciate it if you did (a behavior that makes you feel valued and loved)."

Your power to experience joy and peace in life comes from knowing your worth as God's Creation. The Creator of the Universe LOVES YOU!

When we believe truth, the words we speak create life. They create victory and not defeat. We begin to break off the victim mindset and get into the victory mindset. No weapon [no negative mindset] formed against us will prosper (see Isaiah 54:17)!

*Accept yourself exactly as you are right now. Your thoughts and feelings are valid.

*Journal. Draw. Paint. Find an outlet for what you're thinking and feeling. There are no right or wrong feelings, and there's always a *reason* for them. Ask yourself the reason you think and feel the way you do.

*Be kind and nonjudgmental toward yourself.

*Seek professional help when you need it.

*Avoid getting emotional about other people's opinions of you. No one has any right or place to judge anyone else. Don't use up your valuable energy trying to get acceptance and approval from judgmental people.

*Take responsibility for your thoughts, words, and actions. Apologize when necessary and let people know you're working on changing your thinking and behavior.

*Be patient with yourself and thank people in your life for their patience as well.

*God makes everything beautiful in HIS time (see Ecclesiastes 3:11).

Chapter 13

Why it's Neither Healthy nor Practical to Just Get Over It

Like one who takes away a garment on a cold day, or like vinegar poured on soda, is one who sings songs to a heavy heart.

~Proverbs 25:20

One of the most annoying things I hear people tell those who are suffering is, "Just get over it," or, "Live in the now," or, "Why can't you just let it go?"

The reason we can't "just let go" of our pasts is because our current mindsets, feelings, thinking habits, and the way we view ourselves and others, are all a result of what has happened to us in our pasts.

Sometimes when people tell us to "just get over it," they're afraid we'll stay stuck where we are, never moving forward. While there's a difference between *processing* our pasts with the goal of healing and *ruminating* (going around in circles-doing the same things, thinking the same things, saying the same things-with nothing changing), it's up to each individual to decide for themselves whether they're processing or ruminating. None of us talk about the thing that happened just to talk about it! We want healing but are unsure how to make sense of the thing, process it, understand how we've been affected, and learn and grow.

Until we face what we feel and think, are aware of the *reasons* for our thoughts and feelings and realize why we see ourselves the way we do, we can't "just let it go." We aren't meant to suffer abuse and trauma then immediately say, "Oh, no problem. I'm just going to forget it happened and live in the now."

Our bodies and our brains don't work that way! We're angry. And we should be. Anger protects us and helps prevent further harm. It's not natural or healthy to suffer abuse or a traumatic event and then try to go on with life as if it never happened.

One of the ways our brains and bodies help protect us is by blocking out or disassociating from memories that we don't have the ability to handle or process. A certain sight, smell, sound, or word may make us feel things we don't understand. Be gentle with yourself. Don't think there's something wrong with you. This is the way Our Creator made us.

We cannot heal until we comprehend how we got where we are and we grieve what's been stolen from us-our innocence, sense of self, sense of safety, love, and self-worth.

No one starts to build a house on top of rubble after a tornado has destroyed it. The same is true when we suffer the physical, psychological, and spiritual effects of abuse or trauma. We have to pick through the pieces, deal with the loss, and find a foundation on which to build another house.

Telling someone they shouldn't be a "victim" and they should "just get over it" is like telling them to ignore the damage that's been done and start building something new on top of the debris. It makes no sense in the physical world to do this, and it makes no sense to attempt this mentally or emotionally. We must acknowledge how we were affected before we can develop new ways of seeing ourselves and begin to rebuild.

No one should ever be abused in any way. Loss always occurs when abuse happens. Grieve the losses. Cry; scream; punch a pillow; journal. The emotions must be dealt with. This is a process that can take *years*.

People who tell others not to be a victim or to "just get over it," have already grieved their losses and rebuilt their houses. Or, it's possible that they've never processed their own traumas! Don't listen to these people!

Your journey is your own. No one wants to feel vulnerable, volatile, unsteady, lost, anxious, and unaware of how to move forward. If that's how you feel, know there is hope, but we have to deal with how we've been affected.

Feeling Defeated

A speech teacher in college once told me I project "one-down," or that I present to people that I think of myself as "less than" others. At the time, I didn't understand her meaning, but her statement stayed in my mind for years.

I eventually became aware that I'd adopted this "one-down" demeanor to shrink back and keep from drawing too much attention to myself.

People who've been emotionally abused tend to be happier by themselves-for obvious reasons. Other people have been a source of pain and confusion. And through the lens of emotional abuse, the slightest misstep in a social interaction can be construed as a purposeful intent to harm.

When we see ourselves as "less than," or as a victim, we're subconsciously identifying with defeat, and whether we realize it or not, we're appealing to other people's sympathy to maintain control of their emotions toward us.

I didn't realize I'd been doing this! Once it occurred to me, I became aware that by feeling "less than" others, I wasn't using my God-given power to make my life what I wanted it to be. I was being *reactive* and not *proactive* in life. I was in response mode instead of creation mode!

One reason people who've been abused identify with defeat (or project "one down") is because there's a part of us that thinks we'll be treated better-or at least not blatantly mistreated-if we show we're already downcast.

In other words, if we show we're defeated, other people won't try so hard to hurt us. We've learned that defeating ourselves before someone else has a chance to do it is a way to keep ourselves safe. It's like saying, "You can back off. I've already done the job for you. There's nothing else to do here. You can leave me alone." If the other person sees that we're hurt, then in our minds, we've done to ourselves what they were going to do. A "one-down" mindset makes us feel safe and empowered. It's a subconscious method I used to feel in control of my interactions with people! I knew the way the conversation was going to go. My defeated demeanor guaranteed that I wouldn't leave the interaction feeling any worse than I did before it started! I protected myself from being hurt by the other person by not getting my hopes up. I stayed defeated so that *I* was in control.

I met a young lady who told me her dad treated her kindly only when she wasn't feeling well. She'd developed all sorts of physical ailments. This was the only power she had at the time to influence her environment and protect herself from emotional harm. She remained defeated so that she was in control of how she'd be treated.

Once we're in a safe setting, and we begin to heal, we realize that we don't have to be mistreated. We have a choice about who we want to spend our time with. We start to realize we don't have to feel bad for others to treat us well. We don't have to "earn" the right to be treated appropriately-with dignity and respect.

While a negative mindset is a "victim" mindset, I understand why we develop it! When we're used to things not working out, used to being mistreated, why would we think anything different is possible?

Beginning to Identify with Victory

This is where faith comes in. Hebrews 11:1 says, "Now faith is being sure of what we hope for and certain of what we do not see." I wasn't a positive thinker. I'd been accustomed to negative attitudes and experiences, so in my mind, I had every reason to think negative, defeated thoughts! But I *wanted* to be a positive thinker and I had faith and hope deep down that I could be.

Galatians 6:7 says, "…A man reaps what he sows." I began the sowing process with my words. I experienced a spark of hope, an uplifting, in my spirit when I said, "It will all work out," and I wanted more of that spark! Proverbs 16:24 says, "Pleasant words are a honeycomb, sweet to the soul and healing to the bones," and Proverbs 18:21 says, "The tongue has the power of life and death…."

If we want something different in our lives, we have to *create* something different with our words. When I first started speaking life-giving words over myself and my circumstances, I felt a resistance inside because it was so new and different. Life-giving words railed against my normal negative mindset, and it felt wrong to say them! When soil in a garden gets turned over to plant new seeds, it's a hard task. The soil of my mind was getting turned over to accommodate a new way of thinking.

I didn't give up! The seeds of my speech began to take root in my heart and grow into more positive thoughts. In Luke 6:45 Jesus tells us, "For out of the overflow of his heart his mouth speaks." When our words are life-giving, we're using our faith to speak to things that are not as though they were (see Romans 4:17). By so doing, we're calling into existence, or *creating*, what we're believing for.

You want to feel joy? Start saying, "I am joyful." Start thanking God for creative solutions and for meeting all your needs. He makes a way where we don't see a way. He had an answer before we had the problem! Philippians 4:6 says, "Do not be anxious about anything, but in everything, by prayer and petition, with *thanksgiving*, [emphasis added] present your requests to God." Be thankful. Speak life. Watch how your attitude starts to change your outlook.

It's easy to continue to think the same ways we always have, to do things the same way, but when your heart is truly motivated to change, sometimes you have to *fight* for it. What does that mean? It means you speak the Word of God over yourself-*regardless* of what you see or feel. You say about yourself what God says about you. You speak the promises He made to His children because *you* are His child! Ephesians 6:17 says that the Sword of the Spirit is the Word of God. Pick up your Sword and fight with your life-giving words!

What we focus on shows how we view ourselves. Are we identifying with those who fight for what they want by putting their faith into action and speaking life, or those whose heads are down, hung in defeat? You are not pitiful; you are powerful. Take a chance on yourself and start speaking life-giving words. There's a desire in your heart? Believe you can achieve it!

As the saying goes, "You can do anything you put your mind to." This works both ways-either for you or against you. It's your choice. You have the power to *decide* to experience more peace and joy every day by using your words to be thankful and speak God's Word!

In Chapter 12, we talked about how "learned helplessness" can prevent us from taking responsibility for ourselves. Learned helplessness can also cause us to be *reactive* instead of *proactive*, meaning we *wait* for things to happen instead of taking an active role in making our lives what we want them to be.

In her book, *Pep Talk* (2016), Terri Savelle Foy says, "Successful people take a proactive approach to their dreams."[1]

Look at where you've come from. Find out why things affect you the way they do. Face it. Feel it. Absolutely process it. And get outside help when you need it. Then decide what to focus on-what you want your life to look like-and have the hope and faith that life can feel like a gift. You can feel joy and peace. If God can turn around my thinking, giving me grace to feel His peace and joy in my heart, He can do it for you! Don't give up! Keep hoping and have faith in God!

We make progress toward feeling more peace and joy in our hearts *while* we're dealing with the past. It's important to be aware that healing and modifying our thinking is a process that doesn't always occur in a straight line. In other words, there are layers to our grief and our pain. We get through one layer and feel that we've made progress, because we have! But then we discover later that there are additional layers of that same issue to address. It's okay. Be gentle and patient with yourself. We change more and more as we continue to seek God and speak words of life in faith.

2 Corinthians 5:7 says, "We live by faith, not by sight." We may not *feel* what we're saying. We may not *see* what we're saying, but in the unseen realm, the supernatural realm, things are changing for our benefit when we put our trust in Jesus.

It's the same when we start a new exercise plan, or we start eating healthier. We may not see or feel much transformation at first, but on an unseen, cellular level, changes are happening! If we keep being consistent, keep the faith, keep hoping for something better, eventually, we will see in the natural realm the benefits of our labors! It's always encouraging when we see transitions right away. But it's important to keep going and not give up. It can be hard. It's a fight of faith to speak life when it goes against everything we've ever experienced in our lives. It's a fight of faith to keep making healthy choices when results may be taking a little longer than we wanted, but like my husband says, "Anything worth having is worth working for."

This could be your health-mental, physical, spiritual. It could be that relationship you want restored-with your spouse, your sibling, your friend, your child. Keep speaking life and don't give up when it gets hard. Follow the prompts God puts in your heart. These are the things He tells us to do that don't always make sense to our natural minds.

One time, a friend and I weren't getting along well. There was palpable tension between us. I was trying to forgive, and I wanted reconciliation, but I still felt strain in the relationship.

One day I was out walking, and God told me to buy her something and have it sent to her house. I didn't want to! That's how I knew it was God! I did as He told me, but the result didn't occur as soon as I'd hoped. It was many weeks later before I started to feel peace between us. But what did my obedience do? It planted a seed. That seed took a little time to become what it was intended to be, but the gift I gave her became a talking point that reopened our communication with each other.

Find someone who's been where you are and who can encourage you to keep going. There will be days when you need to "take a knee" (another one of my husband's sayings!), meaning take a break. You may need to watch a funny movie and check out for a while. You know you aren't giving up. You're taking time to refresh yourself.

We don't have to think about our problems all the time! Jesus has already solved all of them. He's known the end from the beginning (see Isaiah 46:10). Do we still need to do our part and stay on course with our thoughts, words, and actions? Of course. Does this require being proactive and not reactive? Absolutely. But we're on the winning team when we follow Jesus. The trenches of life can be hard and can make us feel tired and knocked down. But we don't stay down knowing God will get us through. If He brings you to a problem, He *will* bring you through it.

Fight for the changes you want. Zechariah 4:6 says, "'...Not by might nor by power, but by my Spirit,' says the Lord Almighty." What does that mean? It means we aren't fighting alone. When we use *our* words to speak *God's* Word, we have the supernatural provision of God's Holy Spirit. We're not fighting in our own might or power. God is our Team Captain!

Our attitude is a no-nonsense, we-already-know-we're-on-the-winning-team attitude! We don't fight pitifully. We fight powerfully, with the Word of God.

This isn't said to shame anyone who doesn't feel powerful. This is said to encourage you in the Lord. You are a child of the King of kings and Lord of lords. No weapon formed against you shall prosper (see Isaiah 54:17).

Speak the above scriptures over yourself and your family. Keep your faith and rest in Jesus. He's already won the war. Our battles are meant to make us stronger in Him. Fight like a winner! Fight like you're on the winning team because with your faith in Jesus, you are!

One reason I love sports, whether you compete against another team or against your own personal best, is that you learn to fight through resistance. You learn to not give up when the battle gets hard. You set goals and you work toward them. Once you're in a safe environment, set a goal to identify with victory and not with defeat!

Mindsets to Move Forward

Only you can decide when you're processing and when you're ruminating. Healing can take *years* and can occur in levels that we experience over our lifetimes. Be patient, kind, and gentle with yourself and if anyone tells you to "just get over it," chances are they're not educated on trauma and/or they've already picked through their own "rubble" and rebuilt their foundation. Your healing is *yours*.

The King James Version (KJV) of Proverbs 23:7 says, "For as he thinketh in his heart, so is he…." We can use our words to change what we think of ourselves. Speaking life-giving words ignites a spark of hope in our hearts that life can be better. We can learn to see ourselves as courageous and proactive instead of defeated and reactive!

Write some affirmations on your mirror so you see them every day. Some examples are:

*I identify with victory and not with defeat.

*All my needs are met according to God's riches in glory (Philippians 4:19).

*I am grateful for what I have.

*I speak life over myself and my loved ones.

*I look for the good in life.

When we proactively praise God, He protects us with a peace and joy only He can give (see Philippians 4:4-7). We know that in Him we're unconditionally loved, accepted, and approved of. With our eyes on Our Creator, we can make the choice to have a positive, upbeat attitude. We can refuse to feel negative, defeated, and downcast by other people's anger and control tactics because we don't look to *people* for approval when we know *God* approves us! We no longer have to protect ourselves with a "one-down" demeanor!

Check your tone of voice. If you sound downcast and defeated like I did, and want to sound more positive and upbeat, look for someone whose tone you'd like to emulate. Just like speaking life-giving words might feel weird and wrong at first, so too will changing your tone of voice. Our tone of voice communicates what we're feeling. If we want to *feel* better, sometimes we have to *act* better first!

A positive, upbeat tone does *not* come naturally to me, so I understand that this is hard work!

A constantly angry tone of voice is a sign that we're stuck in negative thinking, expecting the worst to occur, or we expect people to treat us terribly, because this is what has always happened! Once you're in a safe environment, and have started to heal, notice if you sound angry when there isn't an obvious, present reason for it. Sometimes we have a valid explanation for our anger, and we need to use assertive (not aggressive!) communication to talk about it. Anger isn't good or bad in and of itself, but when we use our anger to send the message, "Look out! I'm on a rampage and I'm going to get my way because I've been done wrong," we're seeing ourselves as defeated and showing that we're expecting a negative outcome! We're also using fear and intimidation to control and manipulate, so we're not taking responsibility for ourselves. Identifying with victory requires that we acknowledge our feelings and take ownership of them instead of scaring others into feeling responsible.

If you find yourself constantly angry without just cause, try speaking life into your circumstances. Romans 8:28 says, "And we know that in all things God works for the good of those who love him, who have been called according to his purpose." Try saying, "I have faith in God that He is working all things out for my good." If we want to feel something other than anger, we have to retrain our brains (and our mouths!) to think and speak life-giving words.

Bessel Van der Kolk (2014) wrote the book, *The Body Keeps the Score: Brain, Mind and Body in the Healing of Trauma.*[2] Based on neuroscience and his years working with those who've suffered abuse and other traumatic events, it's a great foundation for helping to understand more about why we are the way we are.

From that understanding, we can know that what we're feeling is NORMAL for what we've experienced in life. We can have empathy and compassion for ourselves and others, and most importantly, we can stop demonizing mental health by telling people to "just get over it!"

Chapter 14

Normalizing Mental Health

We feel ashamed of ourselves if someone has told us, "You should be ashamed of yourself," and we feel ashamed of ourselves because of how we've been treated-even if words weren't used. (See *Mindsets to Move Forward* in Chapter 6 for examples illustrating how others make us feel shame.) Abuse of any kind makes us feel guilty, humiliated, responsible for other people's moods and behavior, rejected, unworthy, like we have to perform perfectly to be loved, like we don't belong, like we're insignificant.

I used to feel embarrassed about the thoughts and struggles I had. I'd heard many times growing up, "You should be ashamed of yourself!" Mission accomplished! I was ashamed of myself. But the more educated I became about the normal responses of our brains and bodies to chronic stress, abuse, or trauma, I was empowered to have empathy, compassion, and understanding for myself instead of shame.

The truth is that part of the way I learned to think served to protect me from further emotional harm, and part of the way I learned to think was based on lies about who I am and how I deserved to be treated.

I've learned not to feel shame about my state of mental health regardless of what others think. For example, a therapist once called me "codependent." (At this point in the book, I've well covered what that means, and it was an accurate diagnosis!) But back then, I had no idea what "codependent" meant, and it didn't feel good to be labeled.

Mental healthcare professionals need a diagnosis to properly bill insurance and to develop a treatment plan, but realize that your worth and value is not found in a man-made label. No matter what our diagnosis is, we are fearfully and wonderfully made. The Creator of the Universe loves and accepts us *exactly* as we are.

We're not our state of mental or physical health. We are holy, righteous, and redeemed (see 1 Corinthians 1:30), and we're working out our salvation (see Philippians 2:12). The thoughts and behaviors I'd developed were the result of my brain protecting me from further pain. It was the result of my brain doing exactly what God designed it to do in chronic stress. Shut down. Protect. Survive.

If you're angry, it doesn't mean something is wrong with you. It means something is *right* with you! Anger is a *normal* response to abuse or other trauma. When we don't feel safe, we're scared, and anger makes us feel protected. Anger can be awesome. It can motivate us to act when change is needed. It can push us to finish what we started when all we can think about is how easy it would be to quit.

When we're angry, there's always a reason. We take responsibility for our lives when we find the reason and work to change what we have the power to change.

Sometimes we wouldn't describe what we feel inside as "anger." Sometimes what we feel is nothing. Sometimes we feel a constant tension in our upper stomach that feels like a volcano ready to erupt at any second. The latter was my experience well past my teen years. I was in a pervasive state of inner tension-tight jaw, tight shoulders, tight hamstrings and lower back, tension headaches.

I remember talking to an aunt who I felt was trustworthy and asking her if she could relate to what I was feeling. She said, "No." I thought, "Well, super! Back to square one."

What to do with this energy trapped in my body?! It sat there for many more years and there's science to suggest that the stuck energy resulted in my having gallstones.[1]

My gallbladder was removed, but it was never the "bad guy." I'd endured years of emotional abuse, rejection, abandonment, and disapproval. Without a safe outlet for the anger that was designed to protect me from further harm, and without the empowerment that comes from knowing I'm unconditionally loved and approved of by The Creator of the Universe, my body suffered the consequences.

There's been much evidence-based research on the somatic, or bodily, effects of anger. Anger has been shown to play a role in the development of many health problems, from heart disease and diabetes[2] to high blood pressure and strokes.[3]

How great would it be if removing a body part made everything better!

But there was still much work ahead of me.

Seeking Balance

Our bodies are designed to seek what's called *homeostasis*. This term refers to the fact that our bodies function best at a certain temperature, blood pressure, heart and respiratory rates, proper level of electrolytes and many more factors. If we're cold, our bodies shiver to produce more heat. If we're too hot, we sweat. You get the idea!

Holistic medicine looks at the whole person-how the body, mind, and soul all affect each other. If there's a problem in one of these areas, it will show up in the others.

Just as our bodies seek regulation and balance, so too, do our souls. If our souls are hurt and in need of adjustment, our emotions can be messengers that guide us toward the issues we need to resolve to find inner peace.

When we haven't been treated properly in life, the thoughts we develop about ourselves move us away from inner peace. Because of the life-giving (and lifesaving!) potential, I'll say it again: Words have power to give life to the body-or death! Proverbs 16:24 says, "Pleasant words are a honeycomb, sweet to the soul and healing to the bones," and Proverbs 18:21 says, "The tongue has the power of life and death…."

If what's been said, and/or done to us, isn't based in the truth of what God says about us, our souls get misaligned. We start to believe lies and it can make our bodies and minds sick. It's a natural consequence of being treated poorly that we become angry! The words spoken over us or the things that have been done to us have made us feel terrible about ourselves, and we know in the core of our beings that God never intended us to feel terrible about ourselves. Our souls, seeking homeostasis, cry out against the injustice! We're angry! And our anger is justified. Our pain is valid.

In situations of abuse, our life circumstances were such that we couldn't fully express and live out who we are, *but that doesn't change who we are.*

We have an indoor cat, Tom, who we don't allow to roam outside. On several of the occasions he was let out, I had to take him to the veterinarian for various injuries. He's now, strictly, an indoor cat.

Regardless of the parameters we've placed on his existence, he has a drive deep inside to do "cat" things! He knows he wants to hunt birds. It's in his nature. He's never witnessed another cat hunting. His parents weren't around to show him what to do. He has innate, or inborn, knowledge of what he was made for. Something comes alive on the inside of him when he experiences his purpose.

Just as Tom has an inner motivation fueled by his nature, the nature of our souls is that we thrive in the presence of Our Creator. Our souls seek connection with God. We have a divine longing for love, peace, wholeness, joy that can be filled only by Him. James 4:5 says, "…the spirit he caused to live in us envies intensely…." The footnote for this verse states, "…that God jealously longs for the spirit that he made to live in us; or that the Spirit he caused to live in us longs jealously." He made you. He put the desire in your heart to know Him, to be in His presence.

Like our cat who isn't satisfied with dry, man-made cat food, but is only fulfilled by what he was created to eat, so is our soul's thirst only quenched in the presence of Our Creator.

If someone has put unnatural parameters on you-said hurtful things about you, made you feel less-than, made you feel like you should be different somehow, made you feel unworthy of love, ashamed, humiliated-use your words to speak life back into your soul.

Say what God says about you. He said He loves you (see John 3:16). He said you are fearfully and wonderfully made (see Psalm 139:14). He said you are his friend (see James 2:23). He said you are his child (see 1 John 3:1). He said his mercies for you are new every morning (see Lamentations 3:22-23). He said when we put our trust in Him, we are not disappointed (see Isaiah 49:23). Psalm 25:3 says, "No one whose hope is in you will *ever* be put to *shame* [emphasis added] …."

Just as our cat got a little "banged up" when he ventured out into the world, when we lean on our human efforts-controlling and manipulating, trying to be filled by the things of the earth-other people's approval and acceptance, money, fame, status, or when we get knocked around a bit by the hurtful words or actions of others, we can return to the refuge of God in us and be healed by what *He* says about us.

Mindsets to Move Forward

Read your Bible every day. Get to know your Creator.

You are not your mental (or physical) health diagnosis. The mindsets we've come to develop are the natural result of what we've experienced in life. BUT we can put our trust and our hope in our *Supernatural God*, who transcends our limited, physical, and mental states. In His presence, we find life and we find healing.

Feel a flood of life-giving energy enter your spirit when you speak God's Word over yourself. Try the following affirmations:

*God loves me.
*I am fearfully and wonderfully made.
*I am God's friend.
*I am God's child.
*He is merciful to me.
*I trust God and am not disappointed.

Don't worry if you don't feel anything right away. Keep speaking these life-giving words in faith, and eventually, you will begin to believe the truth about who Your Creator says you are!

Chapter 15

Social Anxiety

The National Institute of Mental Health defines social anxiety as an intense, persistent fear of being watched and judged by others.[1]

I started experiencing social anxiety when I was in the second grade. I remember being painfully self-conscious-feeling that people were constantly watching me and making negative assessments about me-because, this had in fact, been my experience with people. As a child, I learned from continuous reprimands that regardless of what I was doing, it wasn't the right thing. I wasn't sitting straight enough; I wasn't sitting with my legs closed; I wasn't doing the right activity at the right *time*; I wasn't doing the right activity the right *way*. My mind was plagued with disapproving thoughts so much that I started to block out other people. I wouldn't look people in the eye. If someone joined me in a room, I wouldn't acknowledge them. I began to retreat into myself, desperately seeking protection from negative judgments.

But the judgments had been made, and I started to believe lies. These lies told me that I wasn't acceptable; nothing I did was right; I wasn't approved of. The biggest lie was that my worth and value was determined by other people's opinions. The majority of the time, those opinions were negative. As a result, I developed a negative self-perception, which is the root of social anxiety. I learned that my value and worth come from outside myself. My self-image was based on the disapproving, angry, and impatient words I'd heard from key people in my life-parents, grandparents, siblings, teachers, friends.

I learned to be externally focused for my sense of self-worth and identity. I remember a time in my life that I was so self-conscious that I worried what people were thinking of me when I was doing normal everyday tasks, such as pumping gas! It's *exhausting* to be endlessly concerned with what others think!

Because I learned that my worth and value come from other people, I desperately needed external approval and validation. But because I can't control what other people think, I was insecure and anxious, afraid of not being liked and accepted. Caring too much about what others thought, I was easily controlled and manipulated.

Sometimes, to keep negative judgments from being made about us, we make judgments about other people. This keeps the focus off us so that we aren't the ones being watched and negatively scrutinized. People who make fun of others to keep negative attention off themselves are like wolves or jackals, laughing and cajoling others of their kind to follow their lead. They're just as insecure and anxious as everyone else, but to keep themselves from being judged, they obnoxiously focus their energy into making others feel less than.

My Experience with an Adult Bully

When I was in nursing school, a male student about half my age, thought it would be amusing to label me as having "flat affect." *Flat affect* is a term used to describe someone's facial expression as unchanging despite emotion and is often associated with people who've faced trauma, are depressed, suffer from schizophrenia, or have autism. So, clearly, people who've gone through, or are going through, difficult life situations and need compassion, empathy, and love!

This boy singled me out and began getting others to follow his lead. The class was behavioral nursing in which several of the above-mentioned conditions were discussed, so the term "flat affect" came up frequently. He developed a habit of saying my name aloud in class any time the teacher mentioned "flat affect." At the sound of my name, laughter rippled through the room as I sat in my chair trying to ignore the comments but feeling like I'd been punched in the stomach every time. The root of my pain and the reason I was so deeply affected is because I felt *ashamed*. I'd been devastated by shame as a child.

I was nearly forty years old when I graduated nursing school. However, the behavior from my cohorts, although many of them were several years younger than myself, transported me right back to my school-aged years when I'd been bullied (and/or "harassed"-regardless of what term the law uses, the effects are the same!) for my appearance or mannerisms and made to feel "less than," not part of the "in-group," unworthy of dignity and respect, made to feel that something was wrong with me, made to feel somehow not as valuable as the "cool kids"-made to feel *ashamed.*

This boy's ridiculous behavior went on for weeks. I didn't know how to handle the comments! I started to *dread* going to class. Inside, many of the feelings I'd experienced in my youth came back and I reverted to identifying as a victim. I felt weak, defeated, and powerless to change my circumstances. Making matters worse, this individual had a group of people "on his side" who, by their laughter, seemed to be in agreement with his assessment of me!

Several years ago, when this took place, I wasn't looking for my peace, safety, and security in my Creator. I was still controlling and manipulating-searching for peace in my human relationships.

On top of the bullying from my classmates, and unbeknownst to me (because I wasn't consciously aware I was doing it), I was *enabling* a loved one to be emotionally abusive. This person had grown accustomed to *my* taking responsibility for the consequences of *their* hurtful words and actions. After their abusive rants (which never happened when I was home), I tried to clean up the emotional mess and broken hearts they'd left behind. In other words, I was protecting this person from the results of their behavior (enabling)! I was stressed and my heart was heavy with worry, sadness, and anger. I was scared about what would happen if I held the person accountable. (I deeply regret being so dependent on this person that I didn't immediately act to change the situation. BUT! I pray that what I've written in this book helps someone have the courage to set boundaries, *get counseling*, hold people accountable [by leaving the relationship-temporarily, or permanently, if necessary!], and take responsibility for *only* what *you* are responsible for!)

I didn't have a firm foundation in my identity as a child of God and I hadn't given my heart to Him. (I'd *accepted* Jesus into my heart, but *giving* Him your heart is a completely different level of freedom!) Because I was externally focused on getting approval from others and was emotionally and mentally vulnerable due to my relationship burdens, I was more susceptible to the negative comments from my classmates.

In hindsight, my experience with this adult bully was beneficial in that I became more aware of the destructive impact bullying can have on children. I was an adult and ended up at my best friend's house in tears! I was impacted deeply because I was reminded of being singled out and criticized about "the look on my face" when I was in elementary and high school. Deep down, I believed there was a bit of truth to his words, and I was again being publicly humiliated and rejected by my peers. I didn't want to be seen as someone who has "flat affect," but I still haven't mastered how to make my face show something different than what I feel inside! (I shouldn't have to!) And of course, I had zero control over whether he chose to stop. His bullying set up a seemingly impossible situation in which I didn't *want* to care what others were thinking of me, but I was reminded of their negative assessments so frequently that I began to wear down.

I share this experience because I want you to know that I know what it feels like. People can be cruel. Strong people can become weakened by intentionally harmful words. I had no choice but to be around these individuals in every class. Imagine a student in elementary, middle, or high school who is required, day in and day out, to be around people who make them feel less than, like an outsider, like they're not acceptable as they are, like they're unworthy of dignity and respect, like they're not valuable like everyone else, like something is wrong with them and they don't belong. If you haven't experienced it, you cannot understand the excruciating pain, loneliness, *shame*, and humiliation bullying can cause. If you've lived through similar encounters or are in a comparable situation now, you are not alone.

Bullying and/or harassment should never happen. Talk to a school counselor, a trusted friend, or an adult who can help you manage the intense and overwhelming feelings that this form of abuse can cause. If you're an adult, talk to your manager, your human resource department, or your union representative. Thankfully, my friend was available to me. She listened without judgment. Having her on my side helped me realize I wasn't alone. I began to imagine her and my family standing behind me, supporting me like a band of superheroes who had my back and would defend me.

With this image in my head, I was able to keep going day by day and get through the class. This was the only class in nursing school in which I failed a test. The stress of the harassment had made it difficult to concentrate and learn new information. Imagine children faced with the chronic stress of bullying! Being rejected by your peer group is difficult and painful regardless of age.

But let me tell you how good God is and that He is, in fact, close to the brokenhearted! During the time I was being harassed, I went to a gym one day and met a lady who was going to start teaching kickboxing classes there. (No, I didn't take kickboxing and beat up my harasser! The thought crossed my mind, but I wanted to graduate nursing school!)

She approached me and asked if I would pose for some pictures she could use to advertise her class. I agreed and she held up the sparring pads and talked me through what she wanted while her son took the photos. When we were finished, she was scrolling through the images, and said, "I like the look on your face here. You look fierce. I'm definitely going to use this one."

Her words were like water to my thirsty soul. I felt hope spark in my heart. Where I'd been disapproved of and rejected, I now felt approval and acceptance. I felt like I *belonged.*

We all need positive, life-giving words, but it's important to know the difference between needing a word of encouragement and *relying on* the acceptance and approval of others. This was a time in my life that I needed that perfectly placed compliment. She had no idea what her words meant to me, but God knew I needed to hear them!

I'm still amused at how my bullying situation was resolved. Another classmate told the boy that I was filing a harassment charge against him (which was not true), but it served to get him to back off!

Unfortunately, some people only respond to fear that they will face an untoward consequence instead of being motivated to change by the fact that their behavior is hurtful or damaging to someone else. Don't be the person who has to feel better by putting others down. Know you are loved unconditionally, accepted, and approved of by The Creator of the Universe-and so is everyone else!

New Self-Image

When we've developed a negative self-perception, are externally focused for our value and worth, or are taking on burdens and responsibilities that are not ours to bear, we disempower ourselves. How? We're searching for our safety, security, and inner peace in other people. In my case of enabling, I thought that if I kept "fixing" the damage they did, they'd eventually change. But because we cannot control other people, we start to see ourselves as victims of our circumstances. Our joy, peace, and mental health has become dependent on how *someone else* chooses to behave.

In the past, key people in our lives *have* victimized us by choosing our circumstances for us and robbing us of our joy and peace. But if we *voluntarily* take ownership of other people's abusive behavior-what *they* are responsible for-we are *freely* giving away our power to feel peace and joy.

We've put ourselves in a no-win situation by allowing another person to dodge the consequences of *their* actions. Of course we feel anxious, defeated, negative, and downcast because we're looking for our safety, security, and inner peace in something we have no control of-other people!

We're not meant to enable others so that they're "let off the hook" and don't face consequences for their behavior, and we aren't meant to caretake people or situations that are not the result of our own doing!

In a disempowered state, we're more vulnerable to those who are determined to make us feel "less than" so they can feel a false sense of worth and value. We remain disempowered *until* we fill our hearts and minds with what Our *Creator* says about us, form a new self-image, and stop taking responsibility for the consequences of other people's behavior!

Consider the following:

Your Heavenly Father knew you before your human parents knew you. In fact, Ephesians 1:4 says, "For he chose us in him *before the creation of the world* [emphasis added] to be holy and blameless in his sight." I am deeply awestruck and amazed at this! The Ancient of Days, the King of kings, Lord of lords, the Alpha and Omega, the Beginning, and the End, the Great I AM, has been present since before the creation of the world-and He chose us in Him. *Before the creation of the world*! This gives me an enormous feeling of stability in My Creator. Talk about a Firm Foundation! What! I could spend all day in wonder and fascination about this! The Lord is, was, and always will be (see Revelation 1:8)!

God gave you a purpose and a destiny. Jeremiah 29:11 says, "For I now the plans I have for you," declares the Lord, "plans to prosper you and not to harm you, plans to give you hope and a future." YOU BELONG!

The English Standard Version (ESV) of John 10:10 says, "The thief [the devil] comes only to steal and kill and destroy. I came that they may have life and have it abundantly."

Part of that abundant life is the fruits of the Holy Spirit. These include love, joy, peace, patience, kindness, goodness, gentleness, and self-control (see Galatians 5:22). This is the divine nature of Christ Jesus. Our human experiences may not have included many of these attributes, but we are worthy of them, and they are made possible in us, because of Christ Jesus.

God showed His unconditional love for us in that He sent His Son to save us from eternal separation from Him. Romans 5:8 says, "But God demonstrates his own love for us in this: While we were still sinners, Christ died for us." We were still sinners (unaware of our divine nature* in Christ Jesus), and He *chose* us. That sounds like approval and acceptance to me! (*See Chapter 18.)

Know what God says about you. Renew your mind daily. Say *out loud*, what God says about you. God says we are made in His image (see Genesis 1:26). He *spoke* the world into existence (see Genesis 1:3-26). His word says *our* words also have creative power-power to give life or death (see Proverbs 18:21).

Choose to speak life over yourself and your loved ones-even if all you feel and see in front of you is darkness, despair, lack of hope. We speak to things that are not as though they were and thereby create life with our faith and the power of our words, because this is what God does and we are made in His image! In Genesis Chapter One, God spoke light into darkness (see Genesis 1:1-3) and Romans 4:17 tells us, "…God…gives life to the dead and calls things that are not as though they were."

Romans 4:18 says, "Against all hope, Abraham in hope believed…," and he received what God had promised him! God promised Abraham that he would be the father of many nations (Romans 4:18), but his human circumstance was such that there was no way naturally, or humanly, possible that he could have children. Romans 4:19 says, "…he [Abraham] faced the fact that his body was as good as dead-and that Sarah's [his wife's] womb was also dead." BUT Abraham knew that he served a God who speaks light into darkness, gives life to the dead, and calls things that are not as though they were!

Our faith in Who God is and in who He says *we* are, is what causes our thinking to change. This is how we begin to alter our perception of ourselves. Speaking God's Word over ourselves and our families is how we tear down the lies that have gotten into our hearts.

When negative thoughts start to rattle around in your head, speak a truth about yourself that your *Creator* said. Know that your value and worth come from God and not from humans.

Jesus teaches us in John 8:44, "…for he [the devil] is a liar and the father of lies."

James 4:7 says, "Submit yourselves, then to God. Resist the devil, and he will flee from you. Come near to God and he will come near to you."

How do we resist the devil and his lies? We don't just accept every thought that pops into our heads. We weight our thoughts against the truth of God's Word. And we keep doing it! 2 Corinthians 10:5 says, "…we take captive every thought to make it obedient to Christ."

Make the conscious choice to identify with victory and not with defeat. 1 Corinthians 15:57 says, "But thanks be to God! He gives us the victory through our Lord Jesus Christ." Victory takes root in our spirits when we speak to things that are not as though they are- when we call dead things to life. Negative thoughts and a negative self-perception keep us weak, defeated, powerless and feeling spiritually dead. We call to life that which has been dead by using *our words* to speak *God's Word.*

Know your worth and value is from God, Your Creator, and stop caring so much what other people think. We don't need their approval or validation. God already approved and validated us.

With this in mind, He has approved and validated every other person as well, so we're not to pass judgment on anyone else. People who know their worth is from God, don't have a need to put down anyone else to feel better about themselves. If you catch yourself judging someone, ask yourself if the thing you're judging about them is a thing in you that you're trying to get acceptance and approval for in your own life.

Matthew 7:1-2 says, "Do not judge, or you too will be judged. For in the same way you judge others, you will be judged, and with the measure you use, it will be measured to you."

Knowing we have God's approval, validation, and unconditional love, and continuing to renew our minds to this truth, we empower ourselves to stop worrying what others might be thinking or saying about us. HOWEVER, it is vitally important that we feel safe as we do this work. It is also of utmost importance that we know what we *are*-and what we *are not*-responsible for, and that we are *not* protecting others from the consequences of their actions and thus disempowering ourselves by trying to control what we have no control over-other people's choices! We cannot heal, or create a positive, new self-image, in a toxic, abusive environment-whether that environment is physical (our circumstances) or spiritual (our thoughts). I encourage you to put on the mind of Christ and renew your thinking daily to the fact that you are loved unconditionally and accepted by Our Creator!

Mindsets to Move Forward

For help with bullying, I've included a couple of websites and QR codes below. In addition, the National Mental Health Hotline phone number in the United States is 988.

The first QR code is intended to help school-aged children. Please visit:

https://www.stopbullying.gov/resources/get-help-now

This QR is for adults experiencing workplace bullying. You are not alone. Please visit:

https://www.themuse.com/advice/how-to-deal-with-workplace-bullies

TAKE ACTION

1) Address the harassment immediately. Hold the individual(s) accountable for their intent to harm. Ignoring it will make it worse. Take your children seriously when they tell you they're being bullied at school. Especially for school-aged children, my advice is to aggressively pursue a resolution with teachers and school administrators IMMEDIATELY. If you aren't satisfied with their efforts, consider contacting the ACLU (American Civil Liberties Union), especially in cases of bullying due to race. Your urgent action to end the bullying could literally save a child's life. Get counseling for your child to help improve their self-esteem.
2) Ask for support from people who love you and accept you as you are.
3) Talk to a trusted friend about your feelings.
4) Remind yourself there is no condemnation for those who are in Christ Jesus (Romans 8:1). Another word for "condemn" is "disapprove."[2] God *approves* you!
5) The bully is 100% responsible for their behavior. What they do and say tells who they are, *not* who you are.
6) You are not what others say about you. You are what your Creator says about you.

7) You are unconditionally loved and accepted by The Creator of the Universe, right now, *exactly* as you are.

YOU ARE LOVED

Chapter 16

Not My Circus, Not My Monkeys (Or in This Case, Dog)

One day while I was walking my dog, Patsy, one of my neighbor's pets-a very docile, somewhat goofy dog-began to walk, unaccompanied, with us. This dog had a habit of roaming the neighborhood, but this is the first time it had joined us.

My external control radar immediately started going off and I began to think, "What if this dog gets hits by a car while we're walking?"

My brain, conditioned to be overly responsible and thus controlling, quickly imagined possible scenarios if this event occurred. I would call my husband who would ask his coworker (who knows the dog's owners) what vet they use. I would then heroically (because what value do I have as a person if I haven't done something heroic today?!) load the dog into the back of my car and race off to help save its life!

(To be fair, my intentions wouldn't have been solely to get a pat on the back. This dog is precious, and I want it to stay safe!)

As we continued the walk, I thought, "People are going to think this is my dog, and I'm irresponsibly allowing it to run about the neighborhood unrestrained!" Next thought: If someone thinks the dog is mine and questions the lack of leash, I'll respond by saying, "Why would I have one of my dogs on a leash and one not?" (I know this sounds exhausting. It is! But to maintain clarity of thought, I process what pops into my head so that I'm not held hostage by illogical fear of what people *might* be thinking!)

I kept walking, doing my best to replace my anxious thoughts with peaceful, rational ones. I reminded myself that I have no control over anyone's presumptions.

This did two things: 1) I maintained my inner locus of control by not assuming what anyone else was thinking, and 2) I didn't attempt to control people's judgments of me by offering an unsolicited explanation.

In fact, I told myself, "This is not my circus, not my monkeys!" This saying means that whatever the situation, it isn't mine to take care of! In the days since, I've begun to repeat these words as a mantra when I find myself feeling pulled to control and manipulate or take ownership of circumstances that are someone else's responsibility. Saying the words out loud, "Not my circus, not my monkeys," feels like chains breaking off my mind. It feels incredible to let go of the burden of *over* responsibility! And the fear of not being approved of!

Our approval comes from God. Replacing fearful thoughts with peaceful, logical ones is a practical tool we can access in our daily lives to keep us grounded in that truth and not give away our power by thinking we need external validation-and feeling that we have to control and manipulate to get it.

Additional thoughts/fallacies/mistaken beliefs about this sweet dog were that I was somehow accountable for its safety because it was in my proximity. Not true. Why? I'm not the dog's owner. It would be a different story if I'd made a verbal or written agreement with the owner saying, "Yes. I will dog sit. I will feed, water, and ensure your pet is safe-on a leash-when we take a walk." However, because I'd entered into no such agreement, I wasn't accountable for the dog.

As we continued walking, I began to make a distinction between a natural human response to care about what happens to a living creature and a feeling of *ownership* for its wellbeing. I decided I did care about the dog's safety, but I wouldn't become an anxious mess over what *might* happen.

The thought also occurred to me that I would've taken a completely different stance if I'd come upon someone abusing the dog (or any creature that's not capable of taking care of itself). Proverbs 31:8 says, "Speak up for those who cannot speak for themselves, for the rights of all who are destitute."

The point is, know what you are and are not responsible for and don't feel guilty or obligated to take control. As you begin to implement this into your life, you may find it empowering and fun (!) to say "No" to many requests for your time and talents. Once God starts working to heal our hearts and we're able to distinguish His promptings from accusing voices telling us what we "should" be doing, we'll know when, and to what, to give our time and attention. And the difference is we will *want* to give instead of feeling guilty or ashamed if we do not act.

People who've been raised in controlling, fear-based environments often develop this sense of being overly responsible. We've learned to take ownership of things that are *not* ours to take ownership of, such as other people's moods, behavior, and the consequences of *their* actions. When we're motivated by a sincere desire to give (and not from a need to feel safe, get external approval, or protect others from the consequences of their actions), then we can be *joyful* givers. 2 Corinthians 9:7 says, "Each man should give what he has decided in his heart to give, not reluctantly or under compulsion, for God loves a cheerful giver."

When we've been mistreated and learned that our sense of value and worth or our safety, security, and inner peace is based on what we *do*, we're externally motivated. External motivation is *exhausting*. It places responsibility for our well-being in the hands of another. In this mindset, if we get a pat on the back and told, "Good job," we feel great about ourselves. If our efforts go unnoticed, we don't feel worthy or valued, safe, secure, or at peace. External validation is not a solid foundation. It's shifting sand because you may get the validation you seek or you may not, and if we rely on the approval of others for our identity, we leave our power to feel peace and joy in life in the hands of other humans-not a great idea!

Until we realize that we're unconditionally loved and accepted by The Creator of the Universe, right now, in this very moment, we'll continue to seek external validation. We'll continue to try to prove our worth to others.

I know the emptiness that occurs when your entire worldview shifts, and you realize you don't need external approval. Many of the ways we've interacted with others have been out of fear-fear of not being wanted, loved, or accepted. With this new concept that we're approved of exactly as we are, we need to take time to get to know ourselves outside of fear, anger, and control-that of others and our own.

It can be strange to learn to engage ourselves, and others, from this viewpoint. We begin to see that we're all exactly the same inside. We all have just as much right to be here as anyone else. Regardless of what we have or have not done today, we're all equally, unconditionally loved, and approved of by The Creator of the Universe. God is not a respecter of persons (see Acts 10:34-35), and our worth is not based on our heroic deeds!

Mindsets to Move Forward

Our fear of being judged can become a self-fulfilling prophecy because it shows in our body language. We're anxious and insecure because we're trying to control something we cannot control! People feel (and respond to) our anxious energy*-the nonverbal messages we're sending. The more we care what others think of us, the more vulnerable we feel, and the more negative attention we draw to ourselves because people see that we're easily controlled and manipulated, lacking self-assurance and self-respect. If we don't respect ourselves, others don't either! The bottom line is: when we seek external approval, we leave ourselves vulnerable to negative judgements. (*For the science regarding the effects of our energy on others, see *Mindsets to Move Forward* in Chapter 20.)

But, when we intentionally choose to praise Our Creator, and focus on Him, the vibe we put off is completely different. We enter into God's presence and are *supernaturally* protected by a peace only He can give. Our thoughts are on God, not on fear of what others think, not on our relationship burdens.

Philippians 4:4-7 says, "Rejoice in the Lord always. I will say it again: Rejoice!...Do not be anxious about anything, but in everything, by prayer and petition, with thanksgiving, present your requests to God. And *the peace of God*, which transcends all understanding, *will guard your hearts and your minds* in Christ Jesus [emphasis added]."

Proverbs 4:23 says, "Above all else, guard your heart for it is the wellspring of life." We guard our hearts by keeping our focus on Our Creator. We enter into His protection, His guardianship, when we praise Him, rejoice in Him, and thank Him, knowing we can put our trust in Him.

Psalm 91:1 says, "He who dwells in the shelter of the Most High will rest in the shadow of the Almighty." How do we dwell in His shelter? We praise Him. We keep our minds focused on His unconditional love for us. Verse four of the 91st Psalm goes on to say,

"He will cover you with his feathers and under his wings you will find refuge…."

With these scriptures in mind, we anchor ourselves in the Lord and walk in a peace and protection that only He can give.

When our hearts and minds are focused on praising Our Creator, He hides us under His wings, and He gives us shelter from our enemies. Sometimes our enemy is our own thoughts!

In the presence of God, we realize we don't need to control everyone and everything. Our peace is not outside ourselves! Our peace is in His presence, and in His presence, we know He's got us. In His presence, we know He works all things out for our good (see Romans 8:28).

We don't feel a need to get people to like us or see us in a certain way, and it's because of the workings of our *Supernatural* God. Change doesn't always happen by trying to fix the thing that's broken, using our human ideas and human effort. Change happens when we *trust in Him* and keep our minds on Him. It's not by our might nor by our power, but by His Spirit (see Zechariah 4:6) that we're kept in peace. Exodus 14:14 says, "The Lord will fight for you; you need only to be still." In His presence, we can be still!

This stillness feels like a firm anchor in my heart. His stillness feels like the world could be on fire around me, but I have a peace that passes understanding (see Philippians 4:7). In God's presence, it's just you and your Creator.

In His presence there is no fear, anger, and control. When we finally tire of our human efforts to protect ourselves, lay down our attempts to get external validation (the approval of others), and give our broken hearts to Him, we enter into His protection, His presence, His peace, His love, His light. Matthew 11:28 and 30 says, "Come to me, all you who are weary and burdened, and I will give you rest…For my yoke is easy and my burden is light."

Fear of man comes down to wanting approval from people more than we want to please God. When we've been shattered by disapproval, rejection, or abandonment, this is completely understandable. To begin to rebuild ourselves, we need to fill our hearts and minds with God's Word and the truth of His love for us.

There's a Scripture that strengthens my resolve to please God rather than seek approval from people. In John 12:42-43 we learn, "…many even among the leaders believed in him [Jesus]. But because of the Pharisees they would not confess their faith for fear they would be put out of the synagogue; *for they loved praise from men more than praise from God* [emphasis added]."

Allowing myself to be controlled by the judgments people make of me is like volunteering to be imprisoned. Jesus came to set us free (see Isaiah 61:1)! I have God's approval and there are no chains on me! I don't need people to approve of me. I'm approved of and validated by The Creator of the Universe!

God is for me (see Romans 8:31)!

My prayer is that we will desire the approval of God more than we want to be accepted by people.

Chapter 17

Own Your Power to Make Changes (a.k.a. My Raccoon Rescue)

We aren't meant to solve all our problems in our human strength. The key is knowing what we have the power to change (and owning our power to make the changes!), what only God can do, and when to ask for help from other people or agencies that specialize in the issue we're facing.

In getting help, those of us who've been victims and have felt powerless to change our circumstances in the past need to be aware that we don't give our problem over completely to someone else to fix it. In other words, we don't release all our ownership of the issue, making someone else solely responsible for the solution.

This doesn't mean that we control, manipulate, and tell others how to do their jobs! It means that we advocate for ourselves (or our loved ones who cannot yet advocate for themselves) by asking questions or stating our concerns about what's being done to solve a problem. We continue to recognize our power to use our voice and *we remain accountable for the end result.*

I experienced this one Fall morning almost a decade ago, I was scheduled to attend a college class while my children were out of school for their Fall Break.

It was raining heavily, but I needed to let out our dog, Patsy, to use the bathroom. She finished her business and came around to the back of the house to be let in. I opened the back door and was about to open the screen door when my eyes were quickly drawn to a black figure in the lower left corner. My first thought was, "Oh my gosh! How cute!" Then I thought, "Oh no! What do I do?" It was a young raccoon!

It had climbed through a tear in the screen and gotten stuck between the two doors.

I stepped forward to open the screen door to let it out, but it ran past me and *up the stairs*! My children were up there! I followed the animal, who had climbed onto a bookshelf and was doing its best to conceal itself. I told the kids to stay in their rooms and close the door because there was a raccoon in the house!

(My son, ten years old at the time, drew a map showing the route the raccoon should take to get back outside! My daughter, in her big sister role, helped keep our cat and her brother away from the situation!)

I wasn't sure what the best solution would be as this was a novel scenario, so I called the police department (non-emergency number) to see if they could put me in touch with animal control-people with proper training and equipment!

The dispatcher connected me with animal control. I was relieved a little because I felt one step closer to getting help! But animal control told me to call wildlife experts. I started to think, "This is getting more complicated."

I called the wildlife experts and explained that a young raccoon was in my house and asked what they could do. The lady to me, "Raccoons are 'nuisance' animals. We don't deal with 'nuisance' animals." Then she asked me, "Do you have a computer with internet access?"

Because I was quickly running out of options to resolve this problem, I started to get irritated and worried, and my brain shifted to sarcasm mode. My first thought was, "Why? Do you think the raccoon wants to browse the web?" I only thought it! I didn't say it!

She told me to look up some companies in my area that remove nuisance animals (who knew that was a thing!).

I thanked her for her time and thought, "I have things to do. Who knows how long it will take a nuisance-animal-removal company to get here! My kids are not safe with a raccoon in the house.

They still need to eat breakfast. I've to get to class, and the dog is still outside in the rain! I don't want to wait for someone to come."

So, I wielded my own "nuisance" animal removal equipment in the form of a broom and a lid from a plastic tote. I propped the screen door open and headed upstairs to the bookshelf where this scared, cute, (but possibly dangerous!) raccoon was hiding. I cannot explain how or why this worked, but when I came toward it with the broom (and lid to shield myself!) it ran back down the stairs and out the door! Thank the Lord! It was over!

While I'm pleased with how I handled the above situation (and God's grace to get the animal back outside!), I became aware that in other areas of my life, I had a habit of both, taking *too much* ownership for other people's issues (I protected them from the consequences of their words and actions by trying to fix what they messed up), and I took *too little* responsibility for affecting change regarding things that were important to me.

I noticed that I talked to others about my feelings, concerns, and circumstances, hoping that if I talked to the right person, or enough people, one of them would have a solution for me!

I'd been relying on other people to remedy my problems. (That is, after all, how I learned relationships work. You'll remember from early chapters that my belief was: I fix you and you fix me. Or I'm responsible for you, and you're responsible for me.) Without my awareness, I wasn't owning my power to affect change in my life. I was *talking* about my issues to other people, hoping they would somehow rescue me from my problems. I wasn't doing anything to actually modify my circumstances.

At one point, my family and I were experiencing social injustice and I thought that if I talked about it enough to the right people, change would happen!

Here's what I learned: people don't want to change or implement change on your behalf unless they're personally uncomfortable, or they benefit from it in some way. Other people's hearts are not always broken by the things that break ours.

What's my point? No one is coming to rescue you! If you want change, *you* have to take steps to bring about the transitions.

Part of helping yourself solve your own problems is being aware of resources that are available to you. For example, it shows bravery and accountability when we seek counseling with the attitude that we know we have work to do. We don't go in with the mindset that our counselor is responsible for solving our problems. We go in with the position that they have specialized training and can teach us techniques to empower us. They can help us become more self-aware and give us tools to manage-all with the goal that we take responsibility for *ourselves*.

The bottom line is this: Recognize when you're sharing your problem because you're looking for someone *else* to solve it for you or rescue you. That will never happen! Often only you and the Lord are aware of, or care enough about, the thing that is troubling you to make a change. There's nothing wrong with venting to a friend every now and then *if* we maintain an attitude of empowerment by acknowledging that *we* are accountable for the outcome.

Make sure when you're discussing the burdens of your heart, you're talking to people who can help effect change in your circumstances by 1) holding you accountable for what you're responsible for; 2) pointing you toward resources that will assist you in taking ownership of the issue; 3) giving you practical steps to implement to bring about the modifications you need.

Talking to people who aren't good resources is a way we deny taking responsibility for our problems. I was talking to people about the social injustice we were facing as a family thinking that *they* would do something to remedy it! (One of the people I talked to *was* in a position of authority and could have made a difference, but this person refused to act. I regret not going to the next level of leadership.) Don't make the mistake I did in thinking that others care as much to right social wrongs as you do. If it doesn't affect them personally, why would they care?

For those of you who are social change agents, you get it. You realize that injustice toward one person is injustice toward all. However, some people who aren't held accountable for their actions, or lack thereof, will continue doing what they've always done unless acted upon by a stronger outside force. Don't leave your mental or physical well-being in the hands of people who have demonstrated they will not act in your best interest.

Even when you find people who have the training/information to assist you in your circumstances, *you* are the change agent. The outcome is up to you. Change happens when *you* make decisions, when *you* set new boundaries, when *you* advocate for yourself or your loved ones in the face of injustice, when *you* are brave and honest with yourself about your thoughts and feelings, when *you* have the courage to sit in the discomfort of boundary shifts in relationships and don't give in to fear of making people mad or losing the relationship, or taking responsibility for another person's reaction to *your* new boundaries.

When we've been used to being overly responsible for people's moods and actions, we feel like we're doing something wrong when we enforce boundaries. People are so used to us taking responsibility for them that when we stop, they're in a crisis of identity! They don't know what to do with their emotions if they can't make us take care of them and help them feel better!

In the past we were easily baited by their anger, self-pity, verbal abuse, accusations, their attempts to shame us and make us feel responsible for them. We feel obligated to remedy their mood (because that's what we've always done!) by going back to the way things were so they won't be uncomfortable with the boundary shift.

Because the shift in boundaries is uncomfortable for us too, we think, "I should give in, let them 'off the hook,' continue the way things have been between us because *it wasn't that bad*." God doesn't want us in relationships in which the standard is *it's not that bad*!

He *sacrificed His Son* for us so we could experience *abundant* life-a life of joy, peace, and love-a life with mutually beneficial relationships with healthy boundaries.

Mindsets to Move Forward

Know what you are, and are not, responsible for and own your power to advocate for yourself and your loved ones. Be solution oriented. Even people who are in a position to help may not be able, or willing, to assist you. Don't give up! Go to the next person or governing body in charge. Write to your state representatives. Be a voice that advocates for what you know is right.

Have courage to make the needed transitions in your personal boundaries. Have courage to breathe through the discomfort of a significant other's anger, self-pity, attempts to make *you* feel responsible for *their* behavior. Get support from a friend who understands codependency, can recognize it, hold you accountable for what's yours to take ownership of and point out when you're taking on too much accountability for another person.

If you're acting in self-love by setting a new boundary and are keeping your attitude toward your significant other courteous and professional, YOU ARE NOT DOING ANYTHING WRONG!

Get space as you need it, get support from a counselor, online codependency group, or a friend who has worked through similar issues and place your needs *first*-maybe for the first time ever!

National Domestic Violence Hotline

Available 24/7

Languages: English, Spanish, and over 200 more

1-800-799-7233

thehotline.org

YOU ARE WORTHY TO BE LOVED.

YOU ARE WORTHY OF MUTUALLY BENEFICIAL RELATIONSHIPS WITH HEALTHY BOUNDARIES. YOU HAVE THE POWER TO MAKE CHANGES.

YOU ARE NOT ALONE.

Chapter 18

Sin Nature vs. Divine Nature

"...for all have sinned and fall short of the glory of God."

~Romans 3:23

Having been raised in church, I heard the word "sinner" often. To be honest, I don't like the word! I say this with humility and a reverent fear of God. The reason I don't like the word "sinner" is because it can be a source of guilt, shame, condemnation, and humiliation for those of us who've endured abuse and don't know we're unconditionally approved of and loved by God. No one who feels terrible about themselves wants to come to church and be called a "sinner." It feels like we should be ashamed. It feels like rejection and disapproval.

For us, understanding the term "sin" is confusing. When we've been raised to feel ashamed of ourselves, what was said and done to us was sin! It was wrong, evil, and all the thoughts and reactions we've had because of how we were treated are *completely normal.* With this in mind, it's easy to wonder, "How am *I* a sinner when I'm not the one who did wrong to myself?!"

To reconcile the word "sinner" with a proper view of ourselves, we need to understand that every person has the potential to act in one of two natures-a human nature and a divine, spiritual nature-the nature of Jesus Christ (see 2 Peter 1:4). Every person is capable of the greatest act of love, and everyone has the capacity within themselves to commit the most heinous act.

In Chapter 1 we discussed that we're spirits having a human experience, meaning that our spirits reside within our bodies. 2 Corinthians 5:1 tells us that our bodies are, "…the earthly tent we live in…." Our human nature is referred to in Galatians 5:13 as the flesh, or 'sin' nature, and Galatians 5:17 goes on to say, "For the sinful nature desires what is contrary to the Spirit, and the Spirit what is contrary to the sinful nature. They are in conflict with each other…."

The flesh nature, formed by God of dirt from the earth, desires to do things in our human power. The world tells us our power, our sense of value and worth, comes from external things-what we look like, what we have, or what we can do-what our job title is. Our human nature tells us we get our power by paying back wrong for wrong. Our human nature looks for peace in the drink, the food, the sex, the drugs. Our human nature thinks we have to control and manipulate others to get what we need-to get love, acceptance, and approval. Our human nature is afraid to rely on a power greater than ourselves that we cannot see or touch.

Ability to live in our divine nature is based on our faith in Jesus Christ and the relationship we have with God in our hearts. We cannot see God or touch Him, but we can *feel* Him. We sense when His Spirit urges us to talk to a certain person or to go to a certain place-or, to *avoid* certain people and places! We feel His Holy Spirit comfort us, bringing us peace in chaos-a peace that we cannot rationalize with our human minds-a peace that passes our limited, human understanding (see Philippians 4:6).

When the Bible says that Jesus died for our us while we were yet sinners (see Romans 5:8), it means that He died for us before we knew Him, before we knew we had a *choice* and a hope that we could be anything other than our human nature. His death gave us the option between acting in our flesh or giving our hearts to Him and relying on His power, His Holy Spirit, to work in us.

When He died for us, our human nature (that which makes decisions outside of God's nature), was crucified with Him on the cross, giving us the hope that we don't have to be enslaved by our flesh. We have the choice to accept what He did for us and be led by His Holy Spirit to walk in our divine nature.

Our divine nature, made possible because of Jesus Christ, is that which chooses love over hate, silence over gossip, forgiveness over vengeance. How is it possible to go against our human desires? When we accept Jesus, and give Him our hearts, God sends us The Spirit of His Son (see Galatians 4:6), His Holy Spirit, Who empowers us to make choices that are pleasing to Him. Because of Jesus, we have *supernatural* provision-divine grace-that gives us the power to overcome temptation and walk in God's ways (see 1 Corinthians 10:13). When we give Jesus our hearts, the same Spirit that raised Christ from the dead *lives in us* (see Romans 8:10-11)!

Does this mean we never struggle with our human nature, never slip back into our old habits of thinking and behaving? No. But we become aware of the difference between sinful, human thoughts and actions and those inspired by God's Holy Spirit. When we accept God and give Him our hearts, He promises that He will finish in us the work He started (see Philippians 1:6) which is to removed things in us that don't bring glory and honor to Him! Because of the work Jesus did on Earth (abolishing the power of the flesh nature), He has given us *hope* that we can *be* different and *feel* different. Because of Jesus, we have the capacity to come back to God when our hearts are broken by our behaviors and those of others that don't align with His way.

It means we have a choice, free will, to decide which nature to live in. To experience the abundant life available to us in Jesus, the obvious decision is to live in our divine nature, made possible by giving our hearts to God. Through His Spirit, we have a desire to know Our Creator in a greater way-to cultivate a relationship with Him.

What's our role? Our role is to put our faith into action and follow God's instructions. If we want what He came to Earth to give us, it makes sense that we do what He says! His Word teaches us to set aside the sinful nature and put on the *mind of Christ*. How do we put on the mind of Christ? Romans 12:2 tells us, "Do not conform any longer to the pattern of this world, but be transformed by the renewing of your mind."

By renewing our minds with the truth of God's Word, we're putting on the mind of Christ. The pattern of the world is to live by our flesh. Putting on the mind of Christ means we do what Colossians 3:2 says, "Set your minds on things above, not on earthly things." Why? Verse 3 goes on to say, "For you died, and your life is now hidden in Christ with God." What does it mean, "you died"? It means that when we accept Jesus Christ, our sin nature (the pattern of the world) died and to be "hidden in Christ with God" means that when God looks at us, He doesn't see our sin; He sees his *Son*!

When we accept Jesus, we accept what He did for us, and our human nature is crucified with Him on the cross. We're dead to sin and alive in Christ (see Romans 6:11). Romans 6:6-7 says, "For we know that our old self [the flesh] was crucified with him so that the body of sin might be done away with [rendered powerless], that we should no longer be slaves to sin-because anyone who has died has been freed from sin."

Galatians 5:24 says, "Those who belong to Christ Jesus have crucified the sinful nature with its passions and desires." When we give our hearts to Jesus, we have the *choice* to walk in our divine nature, which is Christ in us. We have the power of God's Holy Spirit to choose what's pleasing to Him.

Every time we choose God's way over our human, natural way of doing things, we crucify our sinful nature. This is what Jesus meant in Luke 9:23 when He said, "If anyone would come after me, he must deny himself and take up his cross daily and follow me." To deny ourselves means we deny acting on the desires of our flesh that don't align with the nature of God.

One of the things that keeps people from coming to Jesus is that we think He's angry with us, and we've dealt with our share of angry people in life! The truth is that God has great compassion and mercy for us (see Nehemiah Chapter 9). It's His kindness that leads us to repentance (to have regret and remorse for sinful actions) (see Romans 2:4). It's His kindness that urges us to turn our *minds* back to Him, renewing our thinking with the truth of His Word. The King James Version (KJV) of Isaiah 26:3 says, "You will keep him in perfect peace whose *mind* [emphasis added] is stayed on you…."

Our Creator knows firsthand how difficult it is to be human and faced with things that threaten to keep us separate from Him (see Hebrews 5:2) because He was fully human (see Colossians 2:9). He suffered every temptation we've ever encountered, and He triumphed over them all (see Hebrews 4:15)! He overcame the flesh/sin nature, the thoughts and actions of which lead to suffering and death, and when we give our hearts to Him, we have the ability to live in His divine nature and experience abundant life! He is worthy of our worship and praise. He is King of kings and Lord of lords. There is no one like Him!

The Nature of God

The Greek word for "sinful" is *hamartolos* which means "to forfeit by missing the mark."[1] What is the mark? The mark, or the standard, is the nature of God. To have His nature, we'd have to match His glory, but Romans 3:23 tells us we've all fallen short of God's glory. By virtue of being human, wrapped in flesh (sin nature), we forfeit having the divine nature of God. This means there's nothing we can do through human effort to become glorified and experience the divine nature of Our Creator.

Only God can, and did, make a way for humans to experience His divine nature. Ephesians 1:4 says, "For he chose us in him before the creation of the world to be *holy and blameless* [emphasis added] in his sight." How? He sent His Son to cancel out our sin nature! The definition of *holy* is dedicated or consecrated to God...sacred.[2] When we put our faith into action, giving Jesus our hearts and accepting what He did for us-dying on the cross to crucify the flesh-our belief in His sacrifice makes us holy and blameless (righteous and justified) in God's sight (see Romans 3:22-24)! And gives us the ability to walk in the divine nature of Our Creator!

Sacred means connected with God.[3] Our human nature, our 'tent of flesh' is referred to in The Bible as the "veil" that *separates* us from God, but Jesus' sacrifice tore that veil (see Matthew 27:51)! Because of Jesus, we get to go 'behind the curtain' (see Hebrews 10:19-21) and enter into the presence of Our Heavenly Father!

Romans 8:17-18 tells us that we *will be glorified* with Christ. When we accept Jesus and give Him our hearts, God sends us His Holy Spirit to begin to work out our salvation (remove things in us that do not glorify Him-things that are contrary to His nature). Because of Jesus, we are *being* glorified and are no longer separated from God by our human, sinful nature! Because of Jesus, we have a *connection* to God!

The God Who Heals the Evil of Abuse

Abuse prolongs our disconnection from Our Creator because the consequences of mistreatment are such that we're stuck in fight or flight with no idea how to begin to heal the traumas we've suffered. We're angry, hurt, fearful, confused, and lost as to how we're to view ourselves. We don't feel unconditionally loved. We don't know how to love ourselves or other people. We feel anger, shame, guilt, lack of self-worth, and humiliation. We control and manipulate to get acceptance and approval, which we've come to view as love. We feel out-of-control inside, unable to be still. We want revenge (at least at first) for what's happened to us, and this is a *completely normal* response and nothing to be ashamed of. God knows what we've been through. He knows how we've been hurt. He doesn't condemn us for the natural responses we've had. In John 3:17, Jesus says, "'For God did not send his Son into the world to condemn the world, but to save the world through him.'"

We're not judged or condemned (disapproved of) for the thoughts and behaviors we've adapted to survive what we've been through in life, but we aren't meant to stay in darkness, thinking we must return evil for evil, controlling and manipulating, looking for our value and worth in the acceptance and approval we get from others.

It's easy to wonder why things happened to us. God hates sin and He hates when evil is done to us, but He gave everyone free will. He wants all of us to choose His way, which was modeled by Jesus, and leads to life and peace. When humans don't choose God's way, the result is *always* pain and suffering.

People who profess to be Christians have a huge responsibility to meet people where they are with love, understanding, empathy, compassion, and non-judgment. Christians must be educated on trauma and stop shaming and demonizing people for the behaviors they've developed to survive the horrors they've been through.

With this in mind, each of us is 100% accountable for how we choose to behave, and for everyone's safety and mental health, we need to operate within boundaries of acceptable actions. Knowing the *reason* for the behavior does not *excuse* the behavior, but we'd all benefit from more grace and understanding. The more educated we are, the less judgmental we are. Hurting people should be able to come to church and not have to hide their pain or pretend to be doing better than they are for fear of being judged, shamed, humiliated, rejected, or told what they "should be" doing!

Jesus is kind, gentle in spirit (see Matthew 11:29), compassionate and empathetic to our suffering (see Hebrews 5:2). He meets our pain with love and not judgement.

God heals and restores us. He responds when we put our faith in Him. In Luke 8:43-48, Jesus healed a woman who'd been bleeding for twelve years because she BELIEVED He could.

Jesus didn't ask her what had caused her problem. He didn't make her confess her sins or state where she'd fallen short of God's glory. He healed her because she reached out to Him and put her *faith* in Him. I imagine that out of her gratitude, her heart was moved by His mercy and compassion, and she WANTED to do right by Him. She *wanted* to walk in His ways. It's the *kindness* of God that draws us to Him (see Romans 2:4). It's His kindness that moves us to repent of our sins (doing things in our human nature that separate us from Him).

It isn't judgement and condemnation that catalyze authentic change and move us into relationship with Our Creator; it's the love and gentleness of Christ.

Mindsets to Move Forward

The truth is God loves us whether we know Him or accept Him. We have a choice: Which nature we nurture determines our quality of life. Whether we *accept* Jesus or *give Him our hearts* (there's a difference!) determines our quality of life! Jesus died to give us life in abundance. John 10:10 (Amp.) says, "…I came that they may have *and* enjoy life, and have it in abundance [to the full, till it overflows]." The fullness of life God came to Earth to give us is available when we make the choice to give Him our hearts.

When we realize that we need a Savior to heal and restore us to God because the sins others have committed against us and our own sin, or human nature, has caused us to be separated from Him, God sends His Holy Spirit to us, and we begin to heal.

Healing is a holy thing, but it isn't always pretty! We have to dig through layers of pain, anger, sadness, confusion, grief, loss, fear, more anger, more sadness. The more layers we peel away and the more hurts we uncover and forgive, the closer we get to a peace that only God can provide.

The point of looking at our pain is to discover the messages we've believed about ourselves. Once we can link what's happened in our lives with our beliefs about ourselves, we can begin to weigh our thoughts against God's Word and replace lies with truth.

The shame of abuse leaves us feeling guilty, unworthy, and rejected. These feelings distort our view of God and our perception of how He sees us. It's difficult to believe we have the potential to be anything other than hurt, scared, angry, confused, and obsessed with revenge. God knew our human desire would be to repay evil with evil. This is the reason Paul reminds us of God's words in Romans 12:19 when he writes, "Do not take revenge, my friends, but leave room for God's wrath, for it is written: 'It is mine to avenge; I will repay,' says the Lord."

When we accept Jesus and give Him our hearts, we have the *choice* to act in His divine nature. He always gives us a way out of temptation. We aren't slaves to the flesh anymore, powerless to choose. The same Spirit that raised Christ from the dead lives in us when we put our faith in Jesus by giving Him our hearts, choosing His way over our human way (see Romans 8:11).

1 Corinthians 10:13 says, "No temptation has seized you except what is common to man. And God is faithful; he will not let you be tempted beyond what you can bear. But when you are tempted, he will also provide a way out so that you can stand up under it."

As humans, we tend to try to fix things about ourselves that only God can change. We hold on tightly thinking we can control the outcome, control others. We put pressure on ourselves to have all the answers. We're inclined to think that if we just keep putting our own human effort into the problem, we can solve it!

Understanding that our thoughts are not God's thoughts, and our ways are not his ways (see Isaiah 55:8), we can cry out to Our Creator and confess to Him that we are limited in our *natural*, human power. Isaiah 55:9 goes on to say, "As the heavens are higher than the earth, so are my ways higher than your ways and my thoughts than your thoughts." We need *Him* to carry the weight of our burdens and restore our souls the way only He has the *supernatural* power to do.

God is in our hearts. To nurture the connection we have with Him, we lay down our human nature and we seek His ways. His way is compassion, mercy, forgiveness-for ourselves and for others.

The evil of abuse is that we haven't felt safe enough to be still. We're constantly on the defensive because we see ourselves negatively and think everyone else does too. We're afraid to trust because no one has shown they're worthy of our trust. But the Bible tells us *not* to trust in mortal men (see Psalm 146:3). Psalm 118:8 says, "It is better to take refuge in the Lord than to trust in man."

To trust God with our hearts, we need to realize God is not natural like humans. God is *supernatural*, able to do exceedingly above all we can ask, or imagine *according to His power that is at work within us* (see Ephesians 3:20). It feels like a risk at first to completely trust God, to let go of wanting revenge, and trying to control and manipulate to get things to go the way we think they should. But there's a peace and freedom that comes when we set aside our human nature and put our faith and trust in Our Creator. Your heart is safe in His hands.

Chapter 19

It's Not About Who We Are or What We've Done; It's About Who He Is

All sin in equal. James 2:10-11 says, "For whoever keeps the whole law and yet stumbles at *just one point* [emphasis added] is guilty of breaking all of it. For he who said, 'Do not commit adultery,' also said, 'Do not murder.' If you do not commit adultery, but do commit murder, you have become a lawbreaker.'" Whether I lied or killed someone, I've sinned and fallen short of the glory of God. There's no such thing as "a little short of His glory."

The Bible says that if we even *think* a sin, it's as if we've committed it in our hearts (see Matthew 5:28). Not one of us can stand in the glory of God. Romans 3:10 says, "There is no one righteous, not even one." Without the sacrifice Jesus made for us, we would be eternally separated from God because of our sin nature.

While each of us is exactly the same inside-all of us human, sinful, and in need of Jesus-some of us have been so harmed by others and so broken that we cover up all ways we feel unworthy. Because we think it's the approval we get from people that makes us valuable, we don't feel safe to admit our flaws, faults, or failures to anyone because we fear judgment and rejection. We're afraid and ashamed.

As Christians, we put pressure on ourselves to keep up outward appearances. In our minds, if we show what we struggle with, we aren't worthy to be called a "Christian."

We hide our true hearts because we've been judged and rejected by key people in our lives. We think we'll continue to be rejected if people see our pain and our anger, so we work and exhaust ourselves trying to prove to others that we're worthy of love and acceptance.

The truth is God sees our hearts and knows us (see Psalm 139:3) no matter how much we cover, disguise, think we're hiding. God wants you to be free from fear of what people think, free from fear of rejection, guilt, and shame. God knows what we've endured in life, and He didn't send Jesus to Earth to condemn us (see John 3:17) or to shame us and disapprove of us. God sent Jesus to show us His unconditional love. He sent Jesus to show us He accepts us and approves of us *as we are*.

As humans, we place different weights on different sins: you lied to the postal worker about what was in your package. You said "no liquids" when you're sending alcohol to your buddy stationed overseas. Maybe not that big a deal to some. Heavier weight: you cheated on your spouse or had impure thoughts of someone. Heaviest weight: you murdered or abused someone.

To God, all sin is the same. It separates us from Him.

Here's the good news. It's not about what we've done. We have ALL sinned and fallen short of God's glory no matter how perfect we look or what we choose to show the world. This may take a minute to digest, but it's the truth. The liar and the abuser are in the exact same boat, along with the murderer and the adulterer. WE ARE ALL THE SAME.

As humans, it's easy to think, "I would never do *that*. What I did is not as bad as what *they* did." You may hesitate and say, "I'm not that kind of person." But we are *all* "that kind" of person. All of us need Jesus. Without Him, we cannot have a relationship with Our Creator.

This is not to say that we don't trust our instincts to stay away from people who are intent on evil. What this means is that we're no different from anyone else. Without Jesus, all of us are separated from God. None of us could stand before Our Creator without the sacrifice Jesus made to atone for our human nature. It doesn't matter if we have no money or all the money in the world. God sees us all the same.

God doesn't show favoritism (see Romans 2:11 & Acts 10:34). He doesn't look at the lie we told and think, "That's no big deal." It's ALL a big deal and until we see that we're all the same, we don't understand what Jesus came to Earth to do. He died for us while we were sinners. He loved us when we were in our sin-while we were slaves to our human nature. He knew everything we would do before we were formed in our mother's womb. And you know what? He made a way for us to get back to Him regardless of what we've done!

Are there consequences for our actions on Earth? Absolutely. Do we have to punish ourselves and stay stuck in guilt and condemnation? Absolutely not. We don't need to feel ashamed of our human nature. But knowing we have a human nature and the divine nature of Christ, we're empowered with awareness to make more conscious choices in our thoughts, words, and actions. We can ask ourselves, "Am I sowing to please my flesh or am I laying down my human desires and making choices that please God?"

What is a choice that pleases God? When I stopped taking my anger out on my family and made the decision to *talk* out my feelings, that was pleasing to God. I chose self-control instead of trying to control others or make them feel responsible for my moods and behavior. We clear the way for God to move in our hearts when we take responsibility for ourselves.

If our hearts are truly repentant, we know what we did was wrong, and we have regret and remorse for our actions. When we ask forgiveness and have no intention of hurting anyone that way again, we can forgive ourselves.

We can have the freedom that Jesus died to give us when we surrender our hearts to Him-admit we need Him and accept Him as our Lord and Savior. Surrendering our hearts to Him means we turn the reigns of our life over to Him. We're no longer trying to control and manipulate other people to get them to change their ways or to get their acceptance and approval. We no longer feel a need to hide, or make up for, our shortcomings. We seek Him first. We read our Bible, go to church, go to counseling. Do the work that's required to heal and get to know who He is. Knowing who He is, we know what He died to give us. When we give Jesus our hearts, He promises in 2 Peter 1:4 that through His glory and goodness, we may participate in the *divine nature*. John 1:12 says, "Yet to all who did receive him, to those who believed in his name, he gave the right to become children of God." As God's children, His promises are for *us*!

We're not our mistakes, our regrets, our pain, or our anger. When we accept Jesus, God sees us as His sons and His daughters. He doesn't see our sin. Romans 8:15 says, "…you received the Spirit of sonship [adoption]."

Our lives aren't over no matter how egregious the infraction was that we committed because, through Jesus, God made a way for us to get back to Him.

In the Bible, King David, Jesus' ancestor, committed adultery with another man's wife then had her husband killed (see 2 Samuel 11). That's a heavy burden. Did that stop God's will and plan for his life? No. Did David struggle with the weight of his sins, like we all have? Yes. Psalms 38 and 51 specifically are the cries of David's soul as he waded through what must have felt like hell on Earth. He was tormented, guilty, ashamed. But he didn't let his guilt and shame keep him from crying out to God. He bore all that was in his heart to God. He wanted reconciliation with his Creator, and He knew Him well enough to know that He restores our souls (see Psalm 23:3).

God wants nothing more than to reconcile our hearts to Him. He hates sin. But He also loves mercy. There's nothing we can do on Earth to pay for our sins. We could serve the time, but that doesn't change what we did. We could apologize to the people we hurt. That doesn't change what we did. NOTHING we are capable of could ever restore our hearts to God or pay for the wrongs we've done. God knew this and that's why He sent Jesus. When we surrender our hearts to Him, give Him all our guilt and shame, all our hurt, anger, and pain, He hears our cries from Heaven and keeps His word: "If we confess our sins, he is faithful and just and will forgive us our sins and purify us from all unrighteousness," 1 John 1:9.

Mindsets to Move Forward

James 5:16 tells us, "…The prayer of a righteous man is powerful and effective." Our first human thought might be, "How do I become righteous so that my prayers will be powerful and effective?!" But it's not about who we are or what we can do in our human strength; it's about Who He is! We're made righteous through our *belief* in Jesus and our *faith to act* on that belief.

In 2 Corinthians 5:21, we learn, "God made him [Jesus] who had no sin to be sin for us, so that in *him* [emphasis added] we might become the righteousness of God."

Habakkuk 2:4 tells us that the righteous live by faith. We demonstrate our faith by giving our hearts to Jesus. When God is in our hearts, His Holy Spirit lives through us and we become the righteousness of God through Jesus Christ! We have access to the divine nature of Our Creator!

The only way a human can be made righteous is by our faith in The Lord Jesus Christ, and by putting our faith into action by giving our hearts to Him.

James 2:19 says that even the demons believe in God. It isn't enough to believe in Jesus, we have to act on our belief and give our hearts to Him. James 2:26 says, "…faith without deeds is dead." We're made righteous only when we believe in Him *and* give Him our hearts. Then He sends His Holy Spirit to work in us. Belief is not enough! If you believe in Him, act on it and give Him your heart.

Only God has the power through Jesus Christ to free us from being enslaved by our human nature. Our role is to seek Him. Read our Bibles, pray, listen to what He tells our hearts. Have faith that when you do these things, God is working in you, and you are changing little by little!

Because I know I cannot earn God's love, but by His divine grace, He loves me, I know that I don't have to prove my worth to anyone else.

Know that judgmental people are not free from their own guilt and fear of rejection and are looking for external approval. People who know Jesus and truly understand our need for Him, know that all sin is equal, *everyone* has fallen short of the glory of God, and we don't need validation of our worth from other humans.

Know that God loves and accepts you exactly as you are as shown in Romans 5:8 which says, "But God demonstrates his own love for us in this": While we were still sinners, Christ died for us."

There is no condemnation (no disapproval) for those who are in Christ Jesus (see Romans 8:1). Say this out loud. Write it down. Hang it on your mirror. Repeat it as often as you need to. Why? Repetition chips away at the lies the devil tries to get us to believe!

The devil uses shame to make us feel weak, defeated, and disapproved of, but God gave us a Spirit of power (see 2 Timothy 1:7).

We are holy, righteous, and redeemed (see 1 Corinthians 1:30).

Hebrews 10:10 says, "…we have been made holy through the sacrifice of the body of Jesus Christ *once for all* [emphasis added]."

We struggle with a proper view of ourselves when others have judged us negatively, rejected us, or held our past sins against us. We fear further judgment and rejection and continue to feel ashamed of ourselves, afraid to talk about our anger, sadness, and pain, but it's vital to remember that what YOUR CREATOR came to Earth to do for you and what *He* says about you overrides *everything* humans have ever said or done. This includes everything *you* have ever said or done! If God says there's no condemnation for those who are in Christ Jesus, then I AM NOT CONDEMNED. I AM ACCEPTED. I AM WORTHY. I AM LOVED.

The world tells us our value is found in external things-our appearance, performance (what we have and have not done), and our possessions. Our true identity, when we accept Jesus and give Him our hearts, is that we're children of God, unconditionally loved by Him.

When we believe Jesus died to free us from our sin nature and we give our hearts to Him, when God looks at us, He sees sons and daughters, heirs of the kingdom of God-not because of who we are or what we've done, but because of what Jesus Christ did for us!

Chapter 20

Authentic Change

People who don't feel good about themselves don't have the capacity to care about others. Why not? You can't pour from an empty cup. You can't export (give to others) what you don't possess, or have, yourself. If we don't love ourselves, we don't have love to give others. 1 John 4:19 says, "We love because he *first* [emphasis added] loved us." We have to be personally familiar with God's love for us before we can truly love others. Our cup has to be filled.

Interestingly, 2 Peter 1:5-7 shows a natural progression of character traits that lead to an understanding of love. Before I gave my heart to God, the words in this passage were beautiful and something to aspire to, but they didn't resonate with me. They were just words. I hadn't experienced their meaning in a personal way.

When I first started controlling my angry behavior, I didn't feel much in my heart. I knew I was wrong, and I wanted to change, but the change wasn't motivated by love at first, because I didn't know how to love! I certainly didn't love myself, and you can't give what you don't have.

2 Peter 1:5 says, "…make every effort to add to your faith goodness." By God's grace, even in the darkest of hells, I've known He's with me. So, to my faith, I added goodness by making the effort to stop taking my anger out on my precious family.

Verse 5 goes on to say, "…and to goodness, knowledge." We gain knowledge of God by seeking Him, reading His Word, and attending a church that teaches from the Bible, telling the truth without guilt, shame, judgment, or condemnation. He always reveals more of Who He is when I read my Bible and seek Him. Have you ever read the same passage multiple times, but when God is ready to reveal something about Himself, the message becomes clear in a way it never was before? That's God keeping His word and rewarding those who seek Him (see Jeremiah 29:13)!

Verse 6 of 2 Peter says, "…and to knowledge, self-control." We talked about self-control in Chapter 2. Authentic control is self-control, which is the empowerment we have knowing that we're unconditionally loved and accepted by God. We don't need external approval and validation from every human we meet, and we don't need to control and manipulate *others* to feel empowered.

Verses 6-7 go on to say, "…and to self-control perseverance; and to perseverance, godliness; and to godliness, brotherly kindness; and to brotherly kindness, love."

As you can see, there are several character traits that start to develop in us as we seek a relationship with God. The more I got to know My Creator, the more I began to notice that I *wanted* to show brotherly kindness to people. My heart began to soften, and I felt the peace of God's love. It wasn't that I set out with a checklist from 2 Peter in hand!

I opened to these verses one day and realized that the traits had begun to take root in my heart as a natural-or more accurately, a *supernatural*-result of seeking God. Authentic change happens from the inside out as God works on our hearts.

The same applies for the fruits of the Spirit-love, joy, peace, patience, kindness, goodness, faithfulness, gentleness, and self-control (Galatians 5:22-23). I used to look at these qualities and think, "How do I get these? How do I show these characteristics in my life?" But we don't acquire things of The Spirit solely through human effort. We change little by little the more time we spend in God's presence. When we seek God first, the kingdom of God within us, all these things are added (see Matthew 6:33).

In seeking God (by reading His Word, spending time alone with Him, attending church), we're putting our faith into *action,* and

He rewards our faithfulness by making Himself known to us in a greater way. He changes things in us we are powerless to change with our limited human ability. Our role is to seek Him, do all we know to do-based on what the Bible tells us-and when we've done that, to stand firm, believing in Him, continuing to put our faith in Him. He keeps His promises!

Galatians 3:3 says, "After beginning with the Spirit, are you now trying to attain your goal by human effort?" In other words, we don't set out *trying* to get the fruits of the Spirit in our human strength. Our human strength is limited and unreliable. Our human strength depends on what mood we're in, or if everything is going smoothly in our lives. When our hearts and minds are set on God, we have *supernatural* provision-His Holy Spirit that works in us to change our hearts. When we seek God, *He* does the work in our hearts that causes the fruits of His Spirit to be produced as a result.

He wants us to lay down our striving, pushing, and controlling and *rest in Him*. When we put our *faith*, our belief, in God, He saves us (redeems us) from our human efforts (see Galatians 2:16 and 3:2). Galatians 3:14 says, "...by faith we...receive the promise of the Spirit."

His will is produced by His peace, not from our pushing. We're to get out of the way (set aside our human, limited agenda) and follow the promptings of His Spirit. In other words, His way is that we deny our desire to control and manipulate people and situations and follow His lead.

His yoke is easy, and His burden is light (Matthew 11:30).

This doesn't make sense to our human mind. We think, "If I don't *try* to get the fruits of the Spirit, how will I get them?" But it's not by might, nor by power, but it's *by His Spirit* (see Zechariah 4:6).

Through Jesus, God has already done the work for our salvation from our human condition. We simply accept what He's done for us and give Him our hearts. I say "simply," but it's hard to let go of control, especially when we've had to protect ourselves, shielding our hearts from evil. But there is a *supernatural protection* that God gives when we keep our focus on Him and His love for us (see *Mindsets to Move Forward* in Chapter 16).

Don't worry if you don't know how to love. There is hope. God is our Healer. Do what you know is right. Keep seeking Him. When you do, He will reveal Himself to you and, eventually, His love will fill your heart.

I Was an Annoying Religious Person

By *religious*, I mean that I wasn't led by The Holy Spirit. I was following man-made edicts (religious rules) that told me what "good Christians" do. I was a Christian who told people what they "should" be doing instead of paying attention to what was going on inside my own heart, but people come more quickly to the conclusion that God's way is best for them when they're free from our judgement, control, and condemnation.

If we tell people what they "should" be doing, and they do it, but it isn't motivated from *inside* of them, they're performing for our acceptance. They're acting to avoid our judgement. They're acting out of fear of shame and rejection. Their actions aren't authentic, and they won't last.

When we aren't internally motivated to act, we aren't telling the truth about what's in our hearts. Avoiding the truth keeps us stuck, hiding, performing for acceptance so we won't be judged and rejected. We experience the breakthrough we need in our lives much more quickly when we don't feel we have to hide our truth.

People are free to be authentic when they know they won't be judged, shamed, condemned, rejected-when they know they're safe.

One of the best catalysts for our freedom is being with those who, instead of telling everyone *else* what they "should" be doing, *they* live what God has put in *their* hearts.

In their presence, we sense their peace and freedom, and it causes something to come alive inside our hearts. Their presence feels like water to our thirsty souls. The Holy Spirit in them connects with the Holy Spirit in us. Psalm 42:7 says, "Deep calls to deep."

Some people think, “But if I know someone isn’t living their life the ‘right’ way-not following God’s ways-how will they know if I don’t tell them?” To answer the question, “They know.” God made us and our souls long for connection with Our Creator (see James 4:5). We may be stuck in pain and hell and not know how to establish the connection, but none of us has a peace that passes understanding without it.

Pointing out that the choices a person is making from their pain and hell are not “right” choices is not helpful. Telling people what they “should” be doing doesn’t address the reasons for the condition of their hearts.

Running around asking people if they know they’re sinners is not helpful. Doing this causes pain and shame.

It's the *kindness* of God that compels us to turn from our sin nature, the desires of our flesh, and follow Him. It’s not guilt, shame, condemnation, control, or manipulation. If people can’t feel the love of Christ in you, you don’t need to try to “win souls to Christ.” If people can’t feel the presence of God when they’re in our presence, our words are not words of love, but of fear, control, and intimidation. If God isn’t moving you to speak, maintain a humble attitude and remain silent. Habakkuk 2:20 says, “But the Lord is in his holy temple; let all the earth be silent before him.” Embrace the beauty of silence and trust God in you to move your heart to speak or act in *His* time. If He hasn't moved you, what's your motivation?

We all need acceptance and approval exactly where we are. God gave that to us (see Romans 5:8), and to follow His way, we demonstrate His love when we accept people as they are. I want my *actions* to show God's love.

Before I knew and felt God's love in my heart, I was a religious person, who feared not doing what I was taught Christians "should" do. I told people about Jesus and pointed out what they were doing wrong in their lives. The message I'd gotten from religion is that we're supposed to "save people from hell."

While I was "saving people from hell" by telling them all the things they "shouldn't" be doing, I was stuck in my own hell.

The most authentic feelings I had were the opposite of love. I was jealous, angry, and kept a record of wrongs (mostly other people's).

My efforts to tell others about God weren't motivated from an overflowing of His love in my heart. I was motivated by fear. As you might imagine, I was the kind of Christian who makes people not want to talk to Christians.

1 John 4:18 tells us, "There is no fear in love. But perfect love drives out fear because fear has to do with punishment. The one who fears is not made perfect in love."

In retrospect, I was working to earn God's acceptance and approval by telling others about Him. Because I didn't know His unconditional love for me, my trying to "save souls" was my *human effort* to make myself worthy of His love! I was performing for God's acceptance and trying to avoid punishment and rejection.

1 Corinthians 13:1-2 says, "If I speak in tongues of men and of angels, but have not love, I am only a resounding gong or a clanging cymbal. If I have the gift of prophecy and can fathom all mysteries and all knowledge, and if I have a faith that can move mountains, but have not love, I am nothing."

Freedom happens inside us and others when we have the courage to tell the truth about where we are-the condition of our hearts.

God's will and purpose in the earth doesn't stop when we take the time we need to do the inner work, the counseling, the digging deep to peel back the layers over our hearts. It's His will that we heal! It's not selfish or self-seeking to do this. We're seeking God's kingdom when we take this time for ourselves because His kingdom is within us (Luke 17:21). We do more to bring Heaven to Earth when we go to God, spend time in His presence, and work from a place of peace than we do by pushing and forcing and acting in fear.

When we're acting in fear, our words and actions are controlling, manipulative, judgmental. Fear leaves people feeling down, depressed, anxious, like energy has been syphoned off them. 1 John 4:18 says, "…fear has to do with punishment…."

Love feels different. 1 John 4:18 also tells us, "There is no fear in love...." Love is uplifting, life giving. Love doesn't leave people feeling guilty, ashamed, condemned, and with the feeling that they have to make up for their mistakes. Love is gracious. (Grace means we don't get what our actions deserve.) Love sets people free. Love covers a multitude of sins (see 1 Peter 4:8). It isn't pointing out our shortcomings that draws us to God. It's His love for us that draws us to Him. His love causes an *internal* motivation that comes from a place of peace and acceptance.

Mindsets to Move Forward

Some of us were taught that self-love is selfish. This isn't true. Why not? God loves us. It makes sense that we would love ourselves! One of the best things we can do is treat ourselves with love-patience, kindness, goodness, gentleness. And GRACE! But we can't export what we don't possess! So, practice being kind and gracious to yourself. Don't say things that put yourself down. Try saying, "I am patience, kindness, goodness, faithfulness, gentleness and self-control-" all the things love is. God is love. He made us in His image, so we can be love too!

Notice when you act out of fear instead of out of love. Ask yourself what you're afraid of. I was afraid I was letting God down by not telling everyone about Him, but because I didn't truly know or feel His love in my heart, I was a clanging cymbal. No one wants to hear that! I was like a cheese grater to human souls-not helpful! Spend time in His presence and you'll begin to heal from shame, guilt, and over responsibility. You'll start to feel His peace and love in your heart.

When we follow His peace and His promptings in us, we do more to bring Heaven to Earth than we could ever do with our limited, human agenda. God has the ability to affect change in others just by our presence. Acts 5:15-16 says, "...people brought the sick into the streets and laid them on beds and mats so that at least Peter's *shadow* [emphasis added] might fall on some of them as he passed by...and *all of them* [emphasis added] were healed."

Based on research conducted by the HeartMath Institute, we know that energy from our hearts is detectable up to three feet away and this energy has an impact on the people around us.[1] An example showing that we respond to other people's energy is shown in The Bible when the woman who'd been bleeding for twelve years touched *the edge* of Jesus' *cloak* (see Luke 8:44), and He said, "...I know that power has gone out from me," Luke 8:46. She touched only his *clothing* and He felt her energy.

Why did Jesus feel only this woman's energy when the crowd was bumping into Him (see Luke 8:45)? She was *expecting* healing and her faith put a demand on Jesus' power that He felt! In other words, she had faith in God as her Healer! When we maintain our relationship with God by seeking Him, reading our Bibles, praising Him, praying, being silent in His presence, we're doing what this woman did. We're reaching out for a touch from Jesus and we're believing in Him for the change we want in our lives and for our loved ones. We're connecting with His *heart*!

After spending time with God, we're prepared to respond when, for example, He urges us to speak to someone. Time in His presence teaches us the difference between a human desire to control and manipulate out of fear and the peaceful urgency of God's Holy Spirit.

If God hasn't moved you to speak, don't underestimate the impact that His love in your heart has on others. We can't export what we don't possess, but we *do* export what we *do* possess. I have an aunt whose presence feels like peace and sunshine. I feel safe, nurtured, and loved when I'm near her even if no words are spoken! If that's not the effect your presence has, don't worry! God uses each of us according to *His* purposes. Trust Him to move your heart if you're meant to speak. But don't underestimate what God does with just your presence!

God has been speaking the word "silence" to me recently. Ecclesiastes 5:2 says, "God is in heaven and you are on earth, so let your words be few." There's a peace in His presence that moves me to be silent and soak it in. There's power in silence. My soul longs for it and I'm filled with gratitude for my Creator.

Psalm 62:1 says, "My soul finds rest in God alone…."

Exodus 33:14 says, "The Lord replied, 'My Presence will go with you, and I will give you rest.'"

Not by might, nor by power, but by His Spirit, He is working in our hearts. Let go of pushing, forcing, fear, control, and manipulation. Embrace silence and find peace and rest in His presence. He keeps His Word. He is worthy of all praise, honor, and glory. Your heart is safe in His hands. Take a deep breath and say, "I trust you, God, to do work in me I could never do on my own."

Rest in Him

Chapter 21

What if What We've Done is so Bad We Can't Forgive Ourselves?

None of us acts in love all the time. We're human. We've been hurt and from our pain, we sometimes hurt others. This isn't said to excuse abusive, harmful behavior. This is said to give hope to those who are truly remorseful because of their actions and want to change. Many times, we don't change until our hearts are broken by what we've done.

If your heart is broken by your actions, you're not alone. The Bible has no shortage of accounts of people who've messed up-committed adultery, murder, carried hatred in their heart toward those who believed in Jesus, and yet they were chosen by God to show His glory-His redemptive power. One of Jesus' ancestors, Rahab, was a prostitute (see Joshua 2:1 and Matthew 1:5) and another was an adulterer and murderer (King David, see 2 Samuel 11:2-4, 14-15 and Matthew 1:6). One of Jesus' disciples, Paul, who was formerly named

Saul, used to hunt, and kill people who believed in Jesus (Acts 22:19-20).

When we're *repentant*, we feel sincere regret or remorse for a wrong[1] we've done. That's a positive thing. Hebrews 12:6 teaches us, "…the Lord disciplines those he loves…." He moves our hearts with the things that move His heart. He breaks our hearts when we haven't acted in love. It's from this place of a broken heart that we begin to change. Because of the pain inside, we don't easily forget our wrong words or actions-the hurt we've caused others. It's from this place of pain and regret that we make the decision to behave differently the next time.

Psalm 34:18 says, "The Lord is close to the brokenhearted and saves those who are crushed in spirit." This means that He's close to us when people hurt us, *and* He's close to us when our hearts are broken by what we've done. Psalm 25:9 says, "He guides the humble in what is right and teaches them his way." When we humble ourselves and admit when we've done wrong, we put ourselves in a position to learn the right way-His way. His thoughts are not our thoughts, and His ways are not our ways (Isaiah 55:8-9). We need Him!

My husband and I once had an argument that occurred because of my misinterpretation of his motives. Something he asked me triggered traumatic times we went through as a family and before I knew it, I'd flashed back to the way things used to be. When emotions had cooled, I realized I'd handled the situation very badly. When old feelings came up and I was feeling triggered, it would've been better for me to take a step back and talk about what was happening inside of me, but instead I reacted to my emotions. I yelled, said hurtful things and the fight got worse.

Even after we apologized to each other, I felt awful inside. I hate that I mishandled my feelings and said hurtful things to my husband. My heart felt down and heavy. My husband forgave me, but I couldn't shake the deep regret and remorse I felt.

How do we move forward when we're truly repentant? We absolutely have to feel the consequences of our actions. That's what motivates us to change, but it was never Our Creator's intention that we stay hurt, broken, and in pain.

God is so gracious. He gently moved me to realize that the conviction I felt inside was because the way I'd treated my husband wasn't in love. When we haven't acted in love, we've separated ourselves from God, Who is love (see 1 John 4:8). 1 Corinthians 13:4-7 says, "Love is patient, love is kind. It does not envy, it does not boast, it is not proud. It is not rude, it is not self-seeking, it is not easily angered, it keeps no record of wrongs. Love does not delight in evil but rejoices with the truth. It always protects, always trusts, always hopes, always perseveres."

How do we reestablish the connection with our Creator when we haven't acted in love? Psalm 22:3 says, "God inhabits the praises of his people," so we begin to praise Him:

God, you are majestic. There is no one like You. You are the King of kings and the Lord of lords. Praise You, God, for sending your Son, Jesus Christ, so I can be brought into your presence by what only He could do for me. I am not worthy of being in your presence without Jesus Christ. Thank you for Who You are and for saving me from sin and death (eternal separation from You) by sending your Son, Who through my acceptance of His sacrifice for my sins (when I don't act in love), allows me to enter into Your presence. Help me take a pause next time I feel old thoughts and feelings arise and help me to process them in a way that leaves relationships intact. I love You, Lord and I want my thoughts, words, and actions to be pleasing to You.

It's not about what we've done or what's been done to us; it's about Who He is. Lies will tell you that you don't deserve to praise God because of what you've done. But our sinful nature is the whole reason for Jesus! We couldn't enter into God's presence without the sacrifice Jesus made for our sins. Our human nature, our sin nature, would cause us to be eternally separated from Our Creator, but out of God's mercy, grace, and unconditional love for us, He sent his Son so by accepting what He did for us, we can enter back into His presence.

Don't let shame stop you from praising your Creator after you've made a mistake. It isn't about what we've done; it's about Who HE is. There is no shame, guilt, or condemnation for those who are in Christ Jesus (see Romans 8:1). This doesn't mean we go around purposefully sinning, but we all mishandle situations. We speak and act in ways that aren't loving which causes us to feel separated from God.

To enter back into His presence (to feel His presence in our hearts) we have to be remorseful for what we've done, and work to conduct ourselves in more loving ways next time. God knows when our hearts are truly broken, and He wants us to be in His presence. Lamentations 3:22-23 says, "Because of the Lord's great love we are not consumed, for his compassions never fail. They are new every morning; great is your faithfulness."

We admit when we fail. We humble ourselves and we seek Him. Praise Him for Who He is and that we don't have to stay stuck in pain and hell. He has mercy for ALL our mistakes!

Mindsets to Move Forward

When you feel old thoughts come up that cause intense feelings, let the other person know you need a break to breathe, think, and process-to look at the reason you were affected so strongly. Research shows it takes *twenty minutes* for the stress response to calm after an intense emotional event.[2] Give yourself (and others) the time.

When you feel remorse for your words or actions, ask God and those you've hurt to forgive you. Forgive yourself and begin to praise God knowing you don't have to feel stuck in guilt and shame.

God disciplines those He loves (see Hebrews 12:6). When we hurt because we've hurt others, that's a good thing. This lets us know God's Spirit is living in us and He's guiding us to walk in His way. He loves us so much that He wants us to learn from our mistakes and move forward in wisdom.

We don't have to walk around with our heads down feeling terrible about what we've done. God gives us hope in Jesus Christ that we can return to Him. We may have been weighed down with the same patterns of thought and behavior for years, but when we put our faith in Jesus Christ, we know we don't have to stay trapped going around in circles with nothing changing.

Romans 10:9-10 says, "…if you confess with your mouth, 'Jesus is Lord,' and believe in your heart that God raised him from the dead, you will be saved. For it is with your heart that you believe and are justified, and it is with your mouth that you confess and are saved." That's all that's required to start your relationship with Him.

We can't *earn* God's forgiveness and He knew that! This is the reason He sent the only One Who would be a worthy sacrifice for our sins. The only One Who could take the place of our limited human efforts, His Son, Jesus Christ, Who did the work for us on the cross. With our faith in Jesus, and our truly repentant hearts, we can forgive ourselves.

*The names and identifying characteristics of the individuals in this chapter have been changed to protect their privacy.

Chapter 22

Forgiving Others

A victim doesn't need forgiveness for the evil that was done to them. A victim needs to relearn who they are. The younger we are when we experience evil, the greater the impact on our identity.

"Come to me, all you who are weary and burdened, and I will give you rest."
~Matthew11:28

When we've suffered at the hands of another person, forgiveness can feel like the last thing we want to do. One woman found this especially true when it was her child who had been wronged.

*Tamara's son bravely told her that he'd been molested repeatedly by a woman who used to babysit him when he was in preschool.

Tamara was in shock, disbelief (not that she didn't believe her son, but she was in denial, the first stage of grief). As the reality of what had happened to her child set in, Tamara began to feel as if the trauma had happened to her. She was rattled to her core with anger, regret, self-blame, frustration, hurt, sorrow, and broken heartedness for her son. The innocence that had been stolen from him could not be returned. The trauma he'd endured and how it had impacted on his life was suddenly glaringly clear considering the information he'd courageously shared.

She was consumed with guilt, fantasies of getting revenge, of putting a bullet in the abuser's head, and things far too gruesome to convey here.

Tamara was in hell. She found herself accidentally calling a friend of hers by the name of the woman who had molested her son. (This friend resembled the perpetrator.) She was tormented daily with images of evil.

Tamara dreamed nearly every night of horrible incidents of abuse. She had no peace. She was consumed with sadness, horror, guilt, and concern for her son's healing.

She was exhausted but felt that if she weren't feeling the effects of what he'd been through that she was letting him down-again. She wanted justice for her child, but he was now an adult, so she couldn't file the police report on his behalf. She felt helpless and didn't know how best to aid her son.

In their book, *Healing What's Hidden* (2022), Evan and Jenny Owens talk about the importance of forgiveness.[1] Reading through the book, forgiving was the last thing she wanted to do. How could she forgive a monster who had hurt her son so grievously? Like a knife to his soul, she had stolen his innocence, robbed him of regular childhood development. Forgive? No. She wanted to kill her.

Not immediately ready to forgive, Tamara sat with the idea a few days and talked to God about all her feelings. She'd been raised saying the Lord's prayer, Matthew 6:9-13:

Our Father in heaven, hallowed be your name, your kingdom come, your will be done on earth as it is in heaven. Give us today our daily bread. Forgive us our debts [sins], as we also have forgiven our debtors [those who sin against us]. And lead us not into temptation, but deliver us from evil, for yours is the kingdom and the power and the glory forever.

Praying this prayer and thinking about her own need for Jesus, Tamara knew that it was necessary to forgive. She talked to God about all her feelings-her reservations about forgiving, her desire to kill the woman (He knew what she'd been thinking anyway!), that she desperately wanted justice for what the woman had done.

Her feelings weren't in it to begin with, but Tamara knew it was the right thing to do-to lay all of her burdens, including her unforgiveness, at the feet of Jesus. She visualized herself kneeling at the foot of the cross and giving it all to her Savior. She asked God to help her.

She said the words to God. Tamara said that she forgave the woman for hurting her son. She cried. She released it. She gave it all to God.

This step was the beginning of finding her peace again. The daytime images stopped. The nightmares stopped.

She told me there are still days when the devil reminds her of what happened, and tries to keep her stuck in horror, guilt, shame, anger, and unforgiveness. It's on those days that she reminds the devil, "What you meant for evil, God turns for good. You have no authority here. My son belongs to the Lord Jesus Christ. No weapon formed against us will prosper!"

The Scriptures she often uses to fight are Genesis 50:20, "You intended to harm me, but God intended it for good to accomplish what is now being done, *the saving of many lives* [emphasis added]," and Isaiah 54:17, "no weapon forged against you will prevail, and *you will refute every tongue that accuses you* [emphasis added]."

Tamara's story is made possible only because of God and the power of His Holy Spirit. Forgiveness doesn't make sense to our human minds. We want revenge. We want justice. We want to make right the wrongs humans have committed against us. We want to repay evil with evil. But because of the *supernatural* workings of Our God, when we choose His way, we find peace. We find healing only He can give.

The bottom line is that revenge is sin. It's the human answer to wrongs committed against us. Sin leads to death (Romans 6:23). If we want the abundant, joyful, peaceful life Jesus Christ died to give us, we have to do things His way. If we want to get free from revenge fantasies, flashbacks, and inner turmoil, we have to realize that every single person who walks the face of this earth is the same. We've all sinned and fallen short of the glory of God. In God's eyes, a lie is just as evil as adultery. A murderer is just as guilty as a thief.

Because God is so just and so holy, there's not a person on this planet who hasn't fallen short of His glory. *And* there isn't a person on this planet who has fallen so far that he or she cannot be forgiven. God is not a respecter of persons.

This is a hard truth for some of us to realize, especially when there's a temptation for those of us with issues of self-worth to build ourselves up and think, "I'm not as bad as him. I didn't do *that*." In God's eyes, we're *all the same*. We're all humans in need of a Savior.

This is not to say that there shouldn't be justice for those who commit crimes. This isn't to say that if you or a child you know is in danger, you should stay in an abusive situation or not report the child abuse. Thank God there are services to help people get out of unsafe circumstances!

Don't let anyone convince you that because we're all the same and in need of a Savior that you're "no better" than they are and therefore don't deserve to be treated well. That's a lie from the pit of hell that helps abusers get away with evil. We're all worthy of love. God saw us as so worthy that He sent Jesus to *suffer and die* for our sins so that we could be set free from death (our human nature) and enjoy life more abundantly.

We are precious and valuable in God's eyes, but after experiencing abuse, we need to reshape our self-image to understand how Our Creator sees us. God is the One Who gives us our identity. Our identity is not what our families said about us; it isn't the negative self-talk that tries to creep into our heads; we're not how others treat us. Our identity is separate from any human praise or criticism. Our identity is not what any human has ever said or done to us.

No matter what, we're unconditionally loved by God, and when we accept Jesus Christ into our hearts, God adopts us into His family as *His children.*

His love for us is unconditional, but the quality of life we want to have is determined by whether we choose to walk in our human nature (making sinful choices) or give our hearts to Jesus and make decisions with the mind of Christ (see 1 Corinthians 2:16). In our divine nature-the nature of Christ in us-we're empowered to make Holy-Spirit-led choices that lead to life and freedom from inner turmoil and emotional hell.

Mindsets to Move Forward

The rage you feel about evil that's been done to you or a loved one is valid. It's a righteous indignation. Cry. Scream. Punch a heavy sack. Run. Do what is necessary to find a healthy, physical outlet for your anger. I wish from the bottom of my heart that none of us ever experienced evil.

But God gave humans free will. He is love. He hates evil.

The evil we've endured in life is because human beings chose to follow the desires of their sin nature. God is not to blame for the choices people make. God is not to blame for the evil we've encountered in life.

The Bible makes it unquestionably clear that humans have a *choice* to walk in the nature of our flesh, which is sinful, vengeful, and evil, and leads to death in every way-heart, mind, body, spirit. *Or* we can accept Jesus Christ, give Him our hearts, and have freedom from our sin nature-freedom to make choices prompted by His Holy Spirit, life-giving choices in line with the divine nature of Christ, and made possible *only* because God is alive and working in us.

God knew our first human instinct when someone hurts us, or our precious loved ones, would be to seek revenge. This is why His Word says in Deuteronomy 32:35, "It is mine to avenge; I will repay."

It doesn't make sense to our human minds, but only when we lay down our burdens, our desire for vengeance, our pain, and our rage at the feet of our Savior, can we get freedom from the hell that sin has caused us.

Be honest with God about what you're feeling and thinking. He knows, but we need to talk it out with Him. He is close to the broken hearted. He cares for us more than we can think or imagine.

Practical Help

If your child tells you someone has abused them, do not ask them for details. DO NOT pressure them to talk about it. It is important that someone trained in interviewing children be the one to conduct the investigation.

Go to www.childwelfare.gov for your state's child abuse and neglect reporting contact information. *Follow up with them.* If a social worker or police officer doesn't reach out to you to interview the child, file a police report to get the investigation moving forward.

Let your child know the abuse is NOT their fault and there is nothing they could ever tell you that would make you see them any differently. Assure them that you love them no matter what and let them know with your words and behavior that they have *nothing* to be ashamed of. *They did not do anything wrong.*

Find a counselor who can help your child heal. At the same time, do not neglect your own healing. Get individual therapy to deal with your emotions. Our children's trauma becomes our trauma. Take care of yourself.

It is of crucial importance to understand how trauma affects our bodies and brains. DO NOT bring up the abuse. If your child brings it up, listen without judgment. DO NOT ask them questions about what happened. As Dr. Bessel Van Der Kolk discusses in his book, *The Body Keeps the Score: Brain, Mind and Body in the Healing of Trauma* (2014), there is a wisdom in us that directs our healing process. If someone tries to force the healing from the outside in (by asking questions before we're ready to talk about it), much more damage is done.[2] It is *vital* to allow people to heal in their own time.

Be available if your loved one needs to talk. If they just need you to sit with them in silence, hold that space for them to feel safe with another person. It may seem like you're not doing anything, but for someone who hasn't felt safe, something as simple as a peaceful presence can feel like life-giving water to their soul.

Get educated about trauma, so you can understand the *reason*s for the behaviors you see in the traumatized person. When we know the reasons for the behavior, we can calmly maintain a stance of grace, compassion, and empathy instead of demonizing the behavior and looking to punish instead of knowing how to help heal.

May you know the peace and healing *only* Our Lord Jesus Christ can give-no matter what hell you or your loved ones have lived through. Because of God, THERE IS HOPE. You will get your joy back. You will laugh again. Hang on. Keep going. Keep crying out to Him. *Keep reading your Bible.*

“The Lord is close to the brokenhearted and saves those who are crushed in spirit.”

~Psalm 34:18

“Instead of their shame my people will receive a double portion, and instead of disgrace they will rejoice in their inheritance; and so they will inherit a double portion in their land, and everlasting joy will be theirs.”

~Isaiah 61:7

The above scripture to means that God gives us *double for our trouble*. What does that mean? It means that *only He* can restore to us what evil has stolen and when He restores us, it will be DOUBLE the amount that was taken!

Additional Resource

1in6 is a nonprofit organization that serves male survivors of sexual abuse and their families. Their website offers educational materials, anonymous weekly support groups, survivor stories, and other resources. Please visit https://1in6.org for more information.

YOU ARE NOT ALONE

YOU ARE A PRECIOUS SOUL AND GOD LOVES YOU UNCONDITIONALLY

Chapter 23

Reaching the End of Myself

"I will give you a new heart and put a new spirit in you; I will remove from you your heart of stone and give you a heart of flesh."

~Ezekiel 36:26

There will come a time on your healing journey when you start to feel like you're going around in circles, saying the same things, thinking the same ways, and the same issues keep coming up. At this point, the only way for healing and change to occur is to give it all to Jesus. What does that mean? It means you realize that you've done all you can do. You've faced it all, felt it all, done all *you* can to heal. You've come to the end of yourself.

It's at the end of our human efforts that we recognize we need the divine intervention of a Savior. We see that we can't move forward without Him. He came to give us *abundant* life, to set us free from going around in circles with the same thoughts and actions, and with nothing changing. When Jesus has your heart, He sends His Holy Spirit to live in you and heal you in *supernatural* ways.

Before I gave my heart to Jesus, there were things about me I prayed He'd heal me of and set me free from, but I couldn't do it in my human strength. After receiving His Holy Spirit, and in *His* time, He removed roadblocks in my heart that I couldn't get past without His strength and the power of His Spirit living in me.

When Jesus has your heart, you process your pain with a different perspective. You see yourself as a child of God, unconditionally loved and approved of by *The Creator of the Universe*! John 1:12-13 says, "Yet to all who received him, to those who believed in his name, he gave the right to become children of God-children not born of natural descent...but *born of God* [emphasis added]."

When we accept God, we have the right to be called *His children* and the promises He made to His people in the Bible become His promises for US!

If you've ever wondered, "How can I take a Bible verse and apply it to my life?" That's how! This is the reason it's so important to read our Bibles and spend time in God's presence daily. We must know Him, how He views us, and what His promises are for His people. God's Word is where we find a firm foundation from which we can begin to move forward.

In His Word, we see that we're approved of (see Romans 8:1) and forgiven (see Matthew 6:12). When we follow His Way, we realize that's where freedom is. In Him we have a new identity. In Him, we realize we aren't what others have said or done to us or what we've said or done. We're a new creation (see 2 Corinthians 5:17), and we can begin to identify as someone who is victorious and not defeated-someone who is loved unconditionally-no matter what!

If we don't accept Jesus Christ and the freedom He gives us from our sin nature, God still loves us, but we won't experience the goodness and fullness of life He made available because of His sacrifice. We'll continue to struggle using our human strength-our thoughts, ideas, plans-our efforts to bring about spiritual change. But when we accept Him, we have access to *supernatural* provision.

When God fights for us, the game changes. He's already defeated the devil, our enemy, by dying on the cross to save us from death. He became the payment that was required for our sin-our separateness from Our Creator. He closed the gap between us and God.

Now, because of Jesus, we have a connection to Our Creator. He lives in our hearts when we accept His Son. He whispers to our spirits and guides us.

Fighting alone, in our human strength, is hard, exhausting, and unsustainable. When we've done all we know to do-taken the prescribed medications-which we should! (I've witnessed anti-anxiety/anti-depressant medications help *save lives* and relationships. I praise God for giving people the knowledge needed to make them! How much better are our lives because of this science! Thank you, Jesus!) When we've done the counseling, listened to the preachers, read all the books-but we still feel that something is missing, we've come to the end of ourselves. Our strength is gone. When we're tired of fighting, pushing, straining, at the end of all we know to do, we're finally ready to give our hearts to Jesus. And we continue daily to give our hearts to Him. What does this mean? It means we lay our mess at His feet. We give up the struggle and turn our hearts over to the only One Who can be fully trusted with them-Our Creator.

Knowing He loves me and has the best plan for me, I surrender my striving, my controlling, my going in circles and coming back to the same place. Only *He* can make right what humans have broken.

We humbly recognize we're not meant to walk our path alone. We lay down our pride that tells us things won't go well if we're not controlling and manipulating and we surrender what we think is best to the One Who is able to do exceedingly and abundantly more than *we* can ask or imagine (see Ephesians 3:20)-Our Creator.

The Day Everything Changed for Me

Special note This section is not just about my husband. He could have written the exact same things about me! We *both* spoke and acted in very harmful ways toward each other in the beginning years of our marriage. The pain we caused each other could have destroyed us, and we are where we are (almost twenty-five years later) ONLY because of the grace of God. God changed my husband's heart first. Mine took a little longer to soften.

Neither my husband nor I had a personal relationship with Jesus when we got married. Because I didn't have a relationship with My Creator, I looked to my husband for validation and approval. I needed to control him to feel safe, secure, and at peace because I relied on him for my self-worth!

When we don't have a firm foundation in our identity as children unconditionally approved of and loved by The Creator of the Universe, our worth and value is completely dependent upon how other people treat us.

I allowed my husband's moods, words, and actions to determine how I felt about myself. If he "made me" feel bad, I controlled and manipulated him with my moods and behavior to make him change the way he treated me!

We were both codependent or 1) I wouldn't have looked to him to determine my self-worth and 2) my control tactics wouldn't have worked to get him to change!

While the changes he made were positive, they weren't internally motivated, so 1) I had to keep controlling and manipulating to get him to treat me in ways that made me feel valued and worthy and 2) I continued to make myself overly responsible for his moods, words, and actions (because my inner peace, safety, and security-my self-worth and value-depended on *him*!)

We both made choices in the beginning years of our marriage that made us doubt our trust in each other.

The KJV of 1 Thessalonians 5:22 says, "Abstain from all *appearance* [emphasis added] of evil." We both did evil and gave the appearance of evil-and we (and our children) suffered for it. The doubt in my mind because of his continued *appearance of evil* caused me to think the worst. Not knowing where my husband's loyalty was, I felt enraged, insecure, and helpless.

The fear of abandonment and anger I felt about not being made a priority to my husband were a recipe for me to increase my efforts to control and manipulate him so that I felt safe and secure and had the assurance he wouldn't leave me.

One of the ways I controlled was with anger and unforgiveness.

In my mind, if he knew I was angry, he would treat me right to protect himself from my anger. When you control someone, you can never give them your approval. If you do, they'll stop trying to get it and you don't have control of them anymore. (I'm not saying to do this! I'm saying this is how control and manipulation work!)

My anger was a signal to him that I disapproved of what he was doing. Subconsciously, I thought if I never gave him my approval, he'd never leave me because he'd keep working to get it! (He's always had a good work ethic and doesn't leave jobs unfinished!)

My anger and unforgiveness gave me a false sense of peace and control and were a way I tried to make him *pay* for his wrongs- even after he'd graciously forgiven mine. He'd gotten to a place in his life in which he'd done some internal work and had changed. I could see and feel the change in him, and I was thankful for it, but at the same time, I was upset about how he'd treated me in the past. I felt that I had to hurt him so that he'd continue to prioritize our relationship. I was afraid that if I weren't controlling him, he'd leave me, and I didn't want to experience any more abandonment in life. I controlled and manipulated to ensure he'd stay with me.

He'd given me a sincere apology and his attitude and behavior reflected his heart change, but I wasn't ready to forgive. I needed to process what had happened over the years. I'd built walls around my heart to protect myself, and I had good reason to keep them up. I wanted to know I could trust him. My heart wasn't going to suddenly open because I got an apology!

On the day God set me free from going in circles, I got up-angry as usual-and told my husband I didn't want to go to church with him (because of some minor infraction he'd committed). (We're easily offended when we need to control and manipulate to feel safe! We need the other person to feel *responsible* for offending us so we can control them!)

I sat on the couch and started to write my feelings in my journal. Here's what I wrote:

If I follow this anger, how long will it take before he looks elsewhere-again. He said, 'You seem edgy.' LOL.

The way I see it, he was able to take all the time he needed to deal with his anger about how he perceives I wronged him, but I don't like things messy and uncomfortable and I don't want him to look elsewhere for things he is supposed to get from his wife.

I don't like being angry. But at the same time, I want to be true to myself and I'm not sure I've ever given myself permission to take the time to do that.

I was too busy trying to win him back instead of making him apologize to me for what he did and commanding respect.

I guess my fear is that we wouldn't make it if I took the time I needed to go thru these hard emotions.

How long am I allowed to be angry?

If he admitted what he's done and apologized for it, would it make a difference?

If he did come to me and admit [his wrongs]and he was truly heartbroken about [them], I think it would finally shed light and justify my thoughts and feelings and the dreams and intuitions I've had for the first 15 years and continue to have at times now.

I have been, in the past, in a huge hurry to make things better-put things back to normal and not go thru hard emotions, hard truths-out of fear that we might not make it out with our relationship intact.

I want to be true to myself. I don't want to bury emotions, intuitive dreams, because they are hard.

Is this whole thing about me being true to myself or my wanting him to admit what he's done?

Isn't it the same once we're one and married?

I feel like I can't move forward and truly forgive him if he isn't truthful with me.

The Bible says to confess your sins.

He's never done that besides, 'I'm sorry I failed you as a husband.'

Well, HOW? Tell me exactly what you did!

By your not telling me the truth, I'm not being true to myself by continuing to let on like everything is OK.

How can I forgive you if you never admitted you did anything wrong except for saying, 'I failed you as a husband'?

Well, what exactly does that mean?

I'm tired of pretending I'm fine and not angry with you for the YEARS of emotional, psychological, and spiritual abuse.

I know you've changed and that makes me even more angry because now I look like the bad person for continuing to be angry at you for all the pain you caused me.

You went to MRT [Master Resilience Training] *then came back and were all positive FOR THE FIRST TIME in the history of our relationship, but I was still reeling from all the ways you had ripped my heart out and smashed it with a hammer for so many years.*

Now you get to be happy? Now you get to be positive?

After all the pain you caused me???!!!

So now I'm left with this intense anger at you for getting to be free and happy and positive.

You NEVER ADMITTED to the WRONGS you committed against me and now you suddenly get to be free? And positive? And feel good about yourself?

I don't trust you. I don't trust you to not hurt my feelings when I make myself vulnerable. I don't trust you to not get from other women what you should get from your wife.

Bottom line is, I don't trust you not to hurt me, so I'm constantly on my guard around you.

I don't like to open my heart to you because you hurt me.

You think that only your stories are valid. You brush over mine as if it's a waste of your time....

You never made me a priority unless you wanted [something]. Then you get really sweet and even affectionate.

B/C YOU WANT SOMETHING!!!

How can I forgive someone who never admitted what they did? The same person who made me doubt myself-my gut instincts, my intuition?

Maybe I will never be satisfied with the answers or lack of answers I get because I'm not meant to be fulfilled in this relationship.

*At this point in my writing, I felt something shift deep inside my spirit. It was as if time stood still, and the following revelation occurred to me. I wrote:

Only my relationship with Jesus can make me feel fulfilled and at peace.

I've been looking for peace in places other than Jesus.

When I finished that last sentence, I was in a state of awe and had a sense of urgency in my spirit. Peace and calm flooded my soul, but I also knew I needed to act. It was a life-altering-light-bulb moment when something came alive on the inside of me in a way that I'd never felt before.

I got myself up off the couch and told my husband that I changed my mind, and I did want to attend church with him.

At the end of the church service, the pastor asked people to come to the front if they needed prayer. My heart was ready. I had come to the end of myself. I'd gone in circles and had kept coming up with nothing-no changes-just the same anger, sadness, fear, unforgiveness, and futile attempts to control.

When it was my turn to be prayed for, the pastor said, "Give your heart to Him." My first thought was, "How did he know I wasn't?!" But the pastor knew because that's how God's Holy Spirit works! He gives us words other people need to hear to get free and to be in relationship with Jesus.

Those were the exact words I needed to hear, and you know what? I did give my heart to Jesus that Sunday morning. I laid down my disillusioned need to control others to get peace. I gave my heart to MY CREATOR and from that day on I've been led by God's Holy Spirit to cultivate my relationship with Jesus. Almost three and half decades after learning *about* God in church, I gave Him my heart and started a *relationship* with Him.

I said it before and I'll say it again, there's a difference between knowing *about* God and having a *relationship* with Him. There's a difference between *accepting* Jesus into your heart and *giving* your heart to Him. Our relationship with Jesus truly starts to grow when we come to the end of ourselves and realize our hearts are safe only in His Hands.

Mindsets to Move Forward

Your worth and value is not found in the eyes of any other human-not even your spouse! We're not meant to be fulfilled in *any* of our human relationships. Lasting peace and joy come only from our relationship with Our Creator.

If you're looking to a person to bring you peace, joy, validation, and approval, you're not going to be happy. If your aim is to find someone to fill holes left in your heart by past relationships, you're not going to be happy. Why not? We're not meant to be fulfilled by other humans. Can there be some healing in our relationships? Absolutely, but our spirits long for *God's presence* (see James 4:5). That's the hole we're really trying to fill. We will never get from humans or any other earthly thing what can only be given to us by Our Creator.

Instead of getting stuck in old patterns of thinking that keep you going in circles, tell yourself, "Moving forward!" My grandma used to say, "That's over and done with." Reminiscing about the past and wishing it had been different won't make it any different and it won't prevent you from experiencing pain in the future!

My encouragement not to get stuck in negative thinking is NOT me saying, "Get over it," (see Chapter 13). I don't believe that we can "just get over" something without processing our thoughts and feelings. There has to be a season of healing. My intention is that you be aware of circular thinking and know when it's time to let go of the illusion that your value and self-worth come from other people.

After my husband had apologized and his behavior reflected his heart change, he was different, but I was holding onto the pain he'd caused me to protect myself from being hurt again. I was trying to make him *pay* for his actions by not forgiving him fully. I thought that if I held onto my hurt and anger that I'd be safe from future hurts.

I was using unforgiveness to try to control him because my inner peace, safety, and security depended on how he treated me! As you've read multiple times now, true control is self-control and comes from knowing God loves us unconditionally, and true inner peace, safety, and security come from cultivating our relationship with Our Creator.

I believed in God and confessed Him as my Savior when I was six or seven years old, so I've been sealed with the Holy Spirit (see Ephesians 2:13) since then, but 1 Corinthians 1:18 tells us we are, "...*being* [emphasis added] saved," and Philippians 2:12 tells us to continue to *work out* our salvation. Each of our paths to a relationship with Jesus is different-and is exactly what it should be because God's purpose for us prevails (see Proverbs 19:21). Ecclesiastes 3:11 says, "He has made everything beautiful in its time...."

I had invited Jesus into my heart, but I had not *given* my heart to Him. Once I *gave* my heart to Him, I had more peace and joy than I've ever had. For the first time in my life, I was able to say, "I love you, God," and actually *feel it* deep in my heart.

Only you know when you're ready to give your heart to Jesus. If you've come to the end of all you can do to find peace-you've cried, screamed, yelled, controlled, and you're exhausted; nothing is changing. If you're angry and constantly tense, the only thing left is to give your heart to Your Creator.

Jesus told us in Matthew 11:28-30, "Come to me, all you who are weary and burdened, and I will give you rest. Take my yoke upon you and learn from me, for I am gentle and humble in heart, and you will find rest for your souls. For my yoke is easy and my burden is light."

For God's glory and your freedom in Christ Jesus, I pray you give your heart to Him and feel the peace *only He can give.*

BONUS CHAPTER

Chapter 24

My Solo Beach Trip and How Gratitude Helped Me Get Unstuck

A couple months ago, I was struggling with feeling trapped, stuck, as if I had cabin fever. My family and I had been through several months of very trying and honestly, traumatic, circumstances. I'd left my full-time nursing job and was at home working on this book.

Day after day, I sat at my computer writing with an urgency to complete my project and had set a goal to be finished at a specific time. I wasn't bored!

The transition from away-from-home employment to at-home work was a blessing. I needed to be available for my family, sometimes at a moment's notice. While I was grateful for what I know was the divine provision of God that allowed me to be home, after more than a year, I began to feel like I couldn't breathe. I felt like I was spiritually suffocating.

I didn't have the energy I used to have. I chalked that up to the trauma we'd been through and were still processing. I was regularly attending church and serving on a volunteer team there, but I still felt spiritually exhausted.

Thinking that a change of scenery might help, I went to the beach for a few days with the intention to get quiet and seek God. I traveled by myself, which in itself was a treat! For other moms or caregivers who are used to pouring yourselves into your loved ones, you understand why alone time is so refreshing! The cherry on top of my solo time is that I was going to *the beach*!

Upon arrival, I checked in and walked out by the ocean to enjoy the sunset.

After the sun had disappeared, I went over to a restaurant, ordered, and soaked in the sights, sounds and delicious smells. I finished my meal and got a piece of key lime pie to go. Yum!

When I returned to my room, I opened the sliding glass door on my balcony to listen to the waves. There's something about the salty air and the sound of the ocean that soothes my soul.

It took a couple days for me to really start to process what was going on inside. It occurred to me the second evening that I'd been feeling down for several months. We'd been in response mode for over a year-not knowing what scary event might happen each day. We'd been shaken to our core because of our family circumstances. My nerves were rattled and honestly, I was scared to let go of thinking that I had control of our situation. I'd begun to think that I could make sure everything went well only if I was always present and available. While it was absolutely necessary that I was consistently available for a season, that season was over, and I felt stuck.

By God's grace, my family and I had fought valiantly through our trauma-on our knees, literally crying out to Our Creator for the life of our loved one and for freedom from depression, anxiety, suicidal ideation, shame, rejection. But the battle had taken a toll on me.

When the enemy tries to take the life of one of your family members, you suffer when you see your loved one suffer. The hell your loved one is in becomes your hell. God gave us dreams that showed what was happening in the spirit realm and let me tell you, I've never fought so hard for anything as I did with my prayers for the life of my precious loved one.

Deuteronomy 20:4 says, "For the Lord your God is the one who goes with you to fight for you against your enemies to give you victory."

The fight is bearable when we know we're on the winning team, but that doesn't mean we sit back and expect change when we haven't prayed for change-when we haven't put our *faith into action* and asked God to move. That would be like showing up to your volleyball competition, for example (because I love volleyball!), knowing you're on the winning team, but sitting on the bench expecting the ball to spike itself!

God refines our faith in Him when we're in the fire. He builds our character. His Word says this is the reason for our trials and tribulations-to refine us, to chisel away parts of us that keep us from knowing Him, the parts of us that keep us from relying on Him (see 1 Peter 1:5-6 & Isaiah 48:10). Romans 5:3-4 says, "…suffering produces perseverance; perseverance character, and character, hope."

One of the most important aspects of our journey through hell was that my husband and I kept strife out of our relationship. When I was tempted to be angry and hold a grudge, thankfully, God urged my spirit and told me to reconcile with him immediately. I had to lay down my pride so that God's purpose could prevail in our trial. The devil uses strife to keep us divided, to keep us weak and take our eyes off God.

Maintaining a united front with my husband was vital. When I knew there was tension in our relationship, I went to him and said, "Babe, God has brought us too far for this little thing to come between us." We prayed and God, because He is merciful, compassionate, and forgiving, heard our prayers and gave us His grace to keep fighting.

The nature of the circumstances we endured was such that we didn't know what to expect from day to day. We had moments of respite and felt we could let off the gas a little, relax a little, maybe even laugh or watch a funny movie, but in the pit of hell, when things were at their worst, the reprieve didn't last more than a day and we were right back in the fight.

Somewhere along the way, after the dust had settled, so to speak, and we'd reached a place of stability in our family, I began to feel trapped, stuck, spiritually depleted. To reiterate, I needed my solo beach vacation!

Again, the intention for my trip was to get quiet for God to speak to me. Because He is a good and faithful God, and keeps His Word that says, "You will seek me and find me when you seek me with all your heart," (Jeremiah 29:13), God did reveal to me what I was looking for.

God had been whispering ideas to my spirit the moment I set out on my trip, but I needed something from Him I didn't realize I needed until the last night I was there. Yearning to hear from my Creator, I opened my Bible and began to read:

Psalm 50:14-15, "Sacrifice thank offerings to God, fulfill your vows to the Most High, and call upon me in the day of trouble; I will deliver you, and you will honor me."

Psalm 50:23, "He who sacrifices thank offerings honors me, and he prepares the way so that I may show him the salvation of God."

It was another moment of divine revelation for me, and I realized the reason for the heaviness in my spirit, my exhaustion, my feeling trapped and stuck. After reading these verses, I wrote in my journal, "I have been looking at everything that's *wrong* with us, our family, our situation. Focusing on what we perceive is *wrong* keeps us stuck in what we perceive is *wrong*! We need to focus on what we *do* want, not on what we *don't* want! We need to focus on what is right and the good, positive things in our lives!"

I realized then that somewhere in the battle, I'd lost my habit of being *proactively* grateful, and I needed to reestablish it!

I completely understand that being thankful, or looking at the positive in life, doesn't come easily, especially for those of us who've endured abuse or trauma. We're so used to things going wrong or not working out that we've walled off our hearts and find it more protective to expect the worst so that we don't feel disappointed. Or, we get a false sense of comfort, thinking we have control of things, if we plan for the worst-case scenario. Like I'd started to do, we have a keen eye for everything that needs to change and it's hard to see the positive or good, because in our experience, the positive and good don't last long enough to really relax and enjoy it.

When we've endured abuse or trauma, it feels like we're holding our breath waiting for the next awful thing to happen. We don't trust the times when things seem calm because we don't know when the next attack will come. We want to be positive and upbeat, but that feels like letting our guard down.

The reason it's called a *sacrifice* of thanks is because it goes against our human nature to be thankful. Left on default mode, our minds gravitate toward the path of least resistance-the negative! Positive, thankful thoughts don't just happen. We have to be intentional about setting our minds in that direction.

Being thankful and praising God when we don't know what will happen next can feel like we're being irresponsible. In military terms, it can feel like we're being *complacent*, not doing our part to ensure safety and success. Enduring traumatic times can cause us to slip into the mindset that we always have to be on guard, prepared for the worst. In other words, because of what we've gone through, we've developed the mindset of thinking constantly about how to prepare for what we *don't want* to happen.

Just like our thank offerings are a sacrifice, it's a sacrifice in faith to let go of the belief that we have control. Psalm 50:23 tells us that thank offerings *prepare the way* for God to show us His salvation. When we let go of the belief that we have to be in control of circumstances for things to turn out well, and we thank God, speak His Word, and praise Him, we prepare the way for *Him* to move. We don't need to concern ourselves with what will happen next because *God* prepares the way.

Complaining or Not Looking for the Positive

We may believe that because we're not complaining with our *words* that we aren't complaining, but Paul advises us in Philippians 4:8 to *think* about, "…whatever is true, whatever is noble, whatever is right, whatever is pure, whatever is lovely, whatever is admirable…anything [that is] excellent or praiseworthy…."

We know from Proverbs 18:21 that, "The tongue has the power of life and death…." Because God doesn't want us using our words to create when we don't have the right attitude (because that would lead to death!), He has given us a very memorable, physical example of this spiritual truth in the Book of Numbers.

After God freed the Israelites from slavery in Egypt, they had to walk through the desert on the way to the Promised Land-the land God told His people that they would take ownership of. While God provided for all their needs, the journey to the Promised Land was not physically pleasant and some of the people began to complain or grumble against Moses, who was leading them, and against God, Who was leading Moses.

The people who were complaining had hardened their hearts and had lost sight of the end goal. They were no longer praising God. They were grumbling against Him! The complaining wore on Moses' heart and God didn't want to hear it anymore either because we see in Numbers 16:31, "…the ground under them [the complainers] split apart and the earth opened its mouth and swallowed them…"! God also set fire to 250 of the complainers (verse 35) and sent a plague to kill even more (verse 49)! In Numbers 17:10, God sums up the point that complaining leads to death when He says, "This will put an end to their grumbling against me, *so that they will not die* [emphasis added]."

The Old Testament offers physical illustrations of spiritual truths. Thankfully (for us!), these people who literally *died from complaining* serve to demonstrate how serious it is that we keep our hearts and minds on God and intentionally look for things to be thankful for! Life and death are in the tongue, and thankfulness prepares the way for the salvation of God!

A Note About Hard Times

When someone doesn't feel physically or emotionally safe, they're in survival mode. Their brains and bodies are in a state of fight, flight, or freeze, and they're not able to think logically. This is a time to *be* the Word of God to them; *be* love, *be* patience, kindness, goodness, gentleness. What does that mean? That means you don't preach at them. That means you don't tell them what they *should* be doing. That means you sit quietly with them and *be* a loving, calm presence when they don't have their own sense of inner peace and calm. That means you educate yourself on trauma and *understand the reasons* for the behaviors instead of punishing the behaviors. With an understanding of trauma, you can have compassion, empathy, and understanding for this precious person who is in living hell. It's compassion, empathy, and understanding that will give you a solid ground on which to remain calm in the face of chaos and ultimately help pave the way for healing.

I know firsthand how difficult it is to focus on the good when you're walking through hell. By God's grace, when our family was going through our hardest time, we were able to continue to praise and thank Our Creator for the promises He made us in His Word.

He said in Isaiah 54:17, "No weapon formed against you shall prosper," so we thanked Him for that.

2 Chronicles 20:15 says, "...Do not be afraid or discouraged because of this vast army. For the battle is not yours, but God's." Thank You, Jesus!

Because we'd been taught that words have creative power, we were careful to use our words wisely whenever people would ask us how things were going.

Eventually, toward the end of the toughest part of our hell, God put a picture in my mind regarding our loved one. Whenever I thought of him, I saw a ball of light-like the sun-surrounded by darkness. I didn't know what it meant, but the image God gave me brought comfort to my spirit and helped me rest in Him in an even greater way.

It was a peace that surpassed my understanding of what I was seeing. But I felt it!

A few Sundays later in church, one of the pastors read Psalm 139. Verse 12 says, "even the darkness will not be dark to you; the night will shine like the day, for darkness is as light to you." I knew then the meaning of the image God had given me. With the Bible verse to back it up, I was able to communicate to others the peace that God put in my spirit regarding our circumstances. He is light in darkness! I'm so thankful for those who follow the promptings of God's Holy Spirit and that we have a church home that helps strengthen us. Don't fight alone! Get a church home!

Mindsets to Move Forward

You may think, "How do I remain thankful and speak life while I'm walking through hell on Earth?" We have a choice: be thankful and *prepare the way* for the salvation of the Lord or complain and remain in the suffering, or worse!

It doesn't matter what the thing is you find yourself grateful for; it matters that you're thankful. Are you breathing? That's a big deal! Thank God for your *life*. Thank God that because of Him, we have *hope*. Speak life-over your loved one and your circumstances-in faith. What does that mean, "In faith?" It means that no matter what it *looks* like, thank God for what He is doing in the spirit realm to work all things out for His glory. Romans 4:17 shows us that we serve a God, "…who gives life to the dead and calls *things that are not as though they were* [emphasis added]." In other words, we might look at our circumstances and see a vast army that is bigger and stronger than we are (i.e., anxiety, depression, suicidal ideation). We might look at our circumstances and not see any way things will work out, but God calls things that are not as though they were, and made in His image, we have the power through Jesus Christ to do the same!

It's okay to say, "God, I don't see any way this will work out, but I trust You. You brought us to this, and You will bring us through this. Your Word says that no weapon formed against us will prosper (see Isaiah 54:17) and I believe that, God. Your Word says that your thoughts are not our thoughts, and your ways are not our ways (see Isaiah 55:8), Lord, and I know You are working this whole thing out for your glory. You are a God of the impossible (see Matthew 19:26). You are able to do exceedingly, abundantly above all we can ask or imagine (see Ephesians 3:20), God, and we pray right now that You would cause our loved one to thrive and not merely survive. We pray that You would hide this precious child from his enemies and provide refuge for him under your wings (see Psalm 91:4). We pray that You will satisfy him long life and show him your salvation (see Psalm 91:16). Lord, it's not by our might nor by our power, but it's by Your Spirit (see Zechariah 4:6), Lord, that we know You are working all things out (see Romans 8:28). Thank You for your grace, mercy, compassion, your divine guidance, your peace, and your all-knowing wisdom, as our intention is to shine the light of your love. In Jesus' mighty name we pray. Amen."

When you spend time in God's Word and listen in His presence, you are drawing near to Him and He *will* draw near to you (see James 4:8).

In no way do I dismiss the serious nature of trauma. Like many of you, I've lived it. It's when the worst of it is over that we may notice we're still worried. We may think that if we aren't available to make sure crap doesn't hit the fan that everything will fall apart. Trauma has the tendency to make us feel that if we don't control and micromanage that things won't end well.

The truth is we've never been in control! Yes, you have a role to play, but God has the final say. He's known the end from the beginning and *His* purpose will prevail (see Isaiah 46:10)!

God is in control, *and* He moves us to pray. Philippians 4:6-7 says, "Do not be anxious about anything, but in everything, by *prayer and petition* [emphasis added], with *thanksgiving* [emphasis added] present your requests to God. And the peace of God, which transcends all understanding will guard your hearts and minds in Christ Jesus." Our prayers served to keep our connection with Him as we walked through hell and to keep our minds and spirits in alignment with Him. If our thoughts and words had become negative and complaining, we might still be fighting the same fight and not seeing any relief from our circumstances.

Just like the Israelites in the desert, our complaining would have led to spiritual death and prolonged our journey through our own dry land.

God speaks to things that are not as though they were (see Romans 4:17). Don't keep repeating what you *see* in the natural realm-how bad it *looks*. We walk by *faith*, not by *sight* (see 2 Corinthians 5:7). In faith, we use the Sword of the Spirit to create life in the spiritual realm. The natural realm doesn't change until the spiritual realm changes. God's will is that we use *our words* to shine His truth, to speak *life*. Say, "Our loved one will live and not die. He will live and proclaim what the Lord has done," (see Psalm 119:17)!

One of the biggest tools the devil uses is trying to get our minds going in a negative direction. If our minds start going that way, you might imagine what happens next. We start complaining about everything that is wrong and our *words* start creating death! The devil came to steal, kill, and destroy (see John 10:10). If he can get us to destroy ourselves with our words, we're making his job easy. A fire rises inside me at the thought of that and I am fortified by The Holy Spirit to speak life and be thankful in all things! Even in the darkest of hells, my encouragement is to find things to be thankful for.

Obviously, we won't always be happy. There are hard times in life, and we will feel difficult, unpleasant emotions. We cried and pleaded with God for our loved one. We hurt. We were sad, angry, scared. We had moments our human nature took over. Thoughts of revenge crossed our minds, but we always said, "No matter what, God's got this."

From the firm foundation that God's promises are true, you can feel every human emotion you need to feel and remain firmly anchored in Jesus Christ. You can stand on His Word, praying God's promises over your circumstances. His love, compassion, and mercy is the only way we got through hell.

My prayer for you is that, in faith, you would know that no matter what, God's got your circumstances and God's got you. If He brought you to it, He *will* bring you through it. I pray you seek Him in His Word and speak life into your situation. In faith, thank Him and praise Him. He is a loving Father Who *never* leaves us or forsakes us.

No matter how dark your hell is, even the darkness is as light to Him (Psalm 139:12) and *He is there with you*!

Notes

Chapter 1~Loss of Connection with Yourself

1. Vogel, K. (2022). *What are the long-term effects of chronic stress?* Psych Central. https://psychcentral.com/stress/long-term-effects-of-chronic-stress-on-body-and-mind

Chapter 2~The Chaos Within: Power and Control

1. Routine. (2023). Oxford English Dictionary online. https://languages.oup.com/google-dictionary-en/
2. Van der Kolk, B. A. (2014). *The body keeps the score: brain, mind, and body in the healing of trauma.* New York, Penguin Books, pp. 86-87.
3. Hühne, A., Welsh, D., & Landgraf, D. (2018). Prospects for circadian treatment of mood disorders. *Annals of medicine, 50*(8), 637-654. http://dx.doi.org/10.1080/07853890.2018.1530449 Retrieved from https://escholarship.org/uc/item/71q72955
4. Milne, A. A. (1954). *Winnie-the-pooh.* [Place of publication not identified.] Dutton.
5. Power. (2023). Oxford Languages online. https://languages.oup.com/google-dictionary-en/
6. Control. (2023). Oxford Languages online. https://languages.oup.com/google-dictionary-en/

Chapter 3~Grace for Parenting: Generational Fear & Anger

1. Grace. (2023). Oxford English Dictionary Online. https://languages.oup.com/google-dictionary-en/
2. Repent. (2023). Oxford English Dictionary Online. https://languages.oup.com/google-dictionary-en/

Chapter 4~Echoes from the Past: Reasons for My Behavior

1. Peiting, L. (2021). Coronavirus recovery: breathing exercises. Johns Hopkins Medicine. https://www.hopkinsmedicine.org/health/conditions-and-diseases/coronavirus/coronavirus-recovery-breathing-exercises

Chapter 6~Chipping Away at the Fear of Man

1. Condemn. (2022). Oxford English dictionary online. https://languages.oup.com/google-dictionary-en/

Chapter 7~Turning Inward

1. Johns Hopkins Medicine. (2023). 9 benefits of yoga. https://www.hopkinsmedicine.org/health/wellness-and-prevention/9-benefits-of-yoga
2. Yoga. (2023). Oxford English Dictionary online. https://languages.oup.com/google-dictionary-en/

Chapter 8~Setting Boundaries & Other Bold Words

1. Boundary. (2023). Oxford English Dictionary online. https://languages.oup.com/google-dictionary-en/

Chapter 12~Responsibility

1. Responsibility. (2022). Oxford English dictionary online. https://languages.oup.com/
2. Henley, W. E. (1888). *A book of verses*. London: D. Nutt, pp. 56-57. Retrieved from https://babcl.hathitrust.org/cgi/pt?id=nyp.33433112041938&view–page&seq=76&q1=scroll
3. Quiller-Couch, A. T., ed. (1902). *The oxford book of English verse, 1250-1900*. Oxford: Clarendon Press, p. 1019. Retrieved from https://babel.hathitrust.org/cgi/pt?id=hvd.32044086685195&view=page&seq=1035

Chapter 13~Why It is Neither Healthy nor Practical to Just Get Over It

1. Foy, T. S. (2016). *Pep talk.* Terri Savelle Foy Ministries, TX, p. xviii.

2. Van der Kolk, B. A. (2014). *The body keeps the score: brain, mind, and body in the healing of trauma.* New York, Penguin Books.

Chapter 14~Normalizing Mental Health

1. Early, R. L, Blumer, L. S., Grober, M. S. (2003). The gall of subordination: changes in gall bladder function associated with social stress. *The Royal Society, 271* (7-13). https://www.ncbi.nlm.nih.gov/pmc/articles/PMC1691567/pdf/15002765.pdf
2. Staicu, M. L. and Cutov, M. (2010). Anger and health risk behaviors. *Journal of Medicine and Life, 3* (4). https://www.ncbi.nlm.nih.gov/pmc/articles/PMC3019061/
3. Hendricks, L., Bore, S., Aslinia, D., & Morriss, G. (2013). The affects of anger on the brain and body, *National Forum Journal of Counseling and Addiction, 2*. http://www.nationalforum.com/Electronic%20Journal%20Volumes/Hendricks,%20LaVelle%20The%20Effects%20of%20Anger%20on%20the%20Brain%20and%20Body%20NFJCA%20V2%20N1%202013.pdf

Chapter 15~Social Anxiety

1. National Institute of Mental Health. (2022). *Social anxiety disorder: more than just shyness*. (NIH Publication No. 22-MH-8083). https://www.nimh.nih.gov/health/publications/social-anxiety-disorder-more-than-just-shyness
2. Condemn. (2022). Oxford English dictionary online. https://languages.oup.com/google-dictionary-en/

Chapter 18~Sin Nature vs. Divine Nature

1. Hamartolos. (2021). Bible Hub. https://biblehub.com/greek/268.htm
2. Holy. (2023). Oxford English Dictionary online. https://languages.oup.com/google-dictionary-en/
3. Sacred. (2023). Oxford English Dictionary online. https://languages.oup.com/google-dictionary-en/

Chapter 20~Authentic Change

1. HeartMath Institute. (2023). Science of the heart: exploring the role of the heart in human performance. https://www.heartmath.org/research/science-of-the-heart/energetic-communication/

Chapter 21~What if What We Have Done is So Bad We Can't Forgive Ourselves

1. Repent. (2023). Oxford English Dictionary online. https://languages.oup.com/google-dictionary-en/
2. Schafer, J. Ph. D. (2011). Controlling angry people. *Psychology Today.* https://www.psychologytoday.com/us/blog/let-their-words-do-the-talking/201101/controlling-angry-people

Chapter 22~Forgiving Others

1. Owens, E. & J. (2022). *Healing what's hidden: practical steps to overcoming trauma.* Revell Books.
2. Van der Kolk, B. A. (2014). *The body keeps the score: brain, mind, and body in the healing of trauma.* New York, Penguin Books.

www.ingramcontent.com/pod-product-compliance
Lightning Source LLC
LaVergne TN
LVHW010559100826
845148LV00014B/2774

* 9 7 9 8 9 8 8 3 5 8 4 0 4 *